D1742294

OLD MOORE'S

HOROSCOPE
AND ASTRAL
DIARY

AQUARIUS

OLD MOORE'S

HOROSCOPE AND ASTRAL DIARY

AQUARIUS

foulsham
LONDON • NEW YORK • TORONTO • SYDNEY

foulsham

**The Publishing House, Bennetts Close,
Cippenham, Slough, Berks SL1 5AP, England**

Foulsham books can be found in all good bookshops or direct from
www.foulsham.com

ISBN 13: 978-0-572-03237-1
ISBN 10: 0-572-03237-4

Copyright © 2006 W. Foulsham & Co. Ltd.

A CIP record for this book is available from the British Library

All rights reserved

The Copyright Act prohibits (subject to certain very limited
exceptions) the making of copies of any copyright work or of
a substantial part of such a work, including the making of
copies by photocopying or similar process. Written permission
to make a copy or copies must therefore normally be obtained
from the publisher in advance. It is advisable also to consult
the publisher if in any doubt as to the legality of any copying
which is to be undertaken.

Printed in Great Britain by Cox & Wyman Ltd, Reading, Berkshire.

CONTENTS

INTRODUCTION

Astrology has been a part of life for centuries now, and no matter how technological our lives become, it seems that it never diminishes in popularity. For thousands of years people have been gazing up at the star-clad heavens and seeing their own activities and proclivities reflected in the movement of those little points of light. Across centuries countless hours have been spent studying the way our natures, activities and decisions seem to be paralleled by their predictable movements. Old Moore, a time-served veteran in astrological research, continues to monitor the zodiac and has produced the Astral Diary for 2007, tailor-made to your own astrological make-up.

Old Moore's Astral Diary is unique in its ability to get to the heart of your nature and to offer you the sort of advice that might come from a trusted friend. The Diaries are structured in such a way that you can see in a day-by-day sense exactly how the planets are working for you. The diary section advises how you can get the best from upcoming situations and allows you to plan ahead successfully. There is room in the daily sections to put your own observations or even appointments, and the book is conveniently structured to stay with you throughout the year.

Whilst other popular astrology books merely deal with your astrological 'Sun sign', the Astral Diaries go much further. Every person on the planet is unique, and Old Moore allows you to access your individuality in a number of ways. The front section gives you the chance to work out the placement of the Moon at the time of your birth and to see how its position has set an important seal on your overall nature. Perhaps most important of all, you can use the Astral Diary to discover your Rising Sign. This is the zodiac sign that was appearing over the Eastern horizon at the time of your birth and is just as important to you as an individual as is your Sun sign.

It is the synthesis of many different astrological possibilities that makes you what you are, and with the Astral Diaries you can learn so much. How do you react to love and romance? Through the unique Venus tables and the readings that follow them, you can learn where the planet Venus was at the time of your birth. It is even possible to register when little Mercury appears to be running retrograde, which can explain why you sometimes feel chatty, whilst at other moments you would rather withdraw into yourself. The Astral Diary will be an interest and a support throughout the whole year ahead.

Old Moore extends his customary greeting to all people of the Earth and offers his age-old wishes for a happy and prosperous period ahead.

THE ESSENCE OF AQUARIUS

Exploring the Personality of Aquarius the Water Carrier

(21ST JANUARY–19TH FEBRUARY)

What's in a sign?

Oh, what a wonderful person you can be! Despite a number of contradictions and one of the most complicated natures to be found anywhere in the zodiac, you certainly know how to make friends and influence people. Your ruling planet is Uranus, one of the more recently discovered members of the solar system's family. It rules modern communications, such as radio and television, and also has a response to the recent discoveries of science. It is within the world of 'the modern' that you reside and you have little or no difficulty keeping up with the ever-increasing pace of life.

People naturally like you and it's not surprising. You are open, liberal, and rarely judgmental, and you are often surrounded by deeply original and even eccentric types. Life to you is a storybook full of fascinating tales. Aquarians amass information 'on the hoof' and very little passes you by. Understanding what makes others tick is meat and drink to you and proves to be a source of endless joy. Unlike the other Air signs of Gemini and Libra, you are able to spend long hours on your own if necessary and always keep your mind active.

Aquarians have great creative potential; they are refined, often extremely well educated and they remain totally classless. This makes it easy for you to get on with just about any sort of person and also explains your general success in the material world. You are fascinating, original, thought-provoking and even quite deep on occasions. Matters that take months for others to synthesise, you can absorb in minutes. It is clear to everyone that you are one of life's natural leaders, but when you head any organisation you do so by co-operation and example because you are not in the least authoritarian.

In love you can be ardent and sincere – for a while at least. You need to be loved and it's true that deeply personal relationships can be a problem to you if they are not supplying what is most important to you. Few people know the real you, because your nature exists on so many different levels. For this reason alone you defy analysis and tend to remain outside the scope of orthodoxy. And because people can't weigh you up adequately, you appear to be more fascinating than ever.

Aquarius resources

Your chief resource has to be originality. Like a precious Fabergé Egg you are a single creation, unique and quite unlike anything else to be found anywhere in the world. Of course, used wrongly, this can make you seem odd or even downright peculiar. But Aquarians usually have a knack for creating the best possible impression. The chances are that you dress in your own way and speak the words that occur to you, and that you have a side to your nature that shuns convention. Despite this you know how to adapt when necessary. As a result your dinner parties would sport guests of a wide variety of types and stations. All of these people think they know the 'real you' and remain committed to helping you as much as they can.

The natural adaptability that goes along with being an Aquarian makes it possible for you to turn your hand to many different projects. And because you are from an Air sign, you can undertake a variety of tasks at the same time. This makes for a busy life, but being on the go is vital for you and you only tire when you are forced into jobs that you find demeaning, pointless or downright dull.

All of the above combines to make a nature that has 'resourcefulness' as its middle name. Arriving at a given set of circumstances – say a specific task that has to be undertaken – you first analyse what is required. Having done so you get cracking and invariably manage to impress all manner of people with your dexterity, attention to detail and downright intelligence. You can turn work into a social event, or derive financial gain from your social life. Activity is the keyword and you don't really differentiate between the various components of life as many people would.

Success depends on a number of different factors. You need to be doing things you enjoy as much you can and you simply cannot be held back or bound to follow rules that appear to make no sense to you. You respond well to kindness, and generally receive it because you are so considerate yourself. But perhaps your greatest skill of all is your ability to make a silk purse out of a sow's ear. You are never stuck for an idea and rarely let financial restrictions get in your way.

Beneath the surface

'What you see is what you get' could never really be considered a sensible or accurate statement when applied to the sign of Aquarius. It's difficult enough for you to know the way your complicated mind works, and almost impossible for others to sort out the tangle of possibilities. Your mind can be as untidy as a tatty workbox on occasions and yet at other times you can see through situations with a clarity that would dazzle almost any observer. It really depends on a whole host of circumstances, some of which are inevitably beyond your own control. You are at your best when you are allowed to take charge from the very start of any project, because then your originality of thought comes into play. Your sort of logic is unique to you, so don't expect anyone else to go down the same mental routes that you find easy to follow.

Aquarians are naturally kind and don't tend to discriminate. This is not a considered matter, it's simply the way you are. As a result it is very hard for you to understand prejudice, or individuals who show any form of intolerance. The fairness that you exemplify isn't something that you have to work at – it comes as naturally to you as breathing does.

You can be very peculiar and even a little cranky on occasions. These aspects of your nature are unlikely to have any bearing on your overall popularity, but they do betray a rather unusual mindset that isn't like that of any other zodiac sign. When you feel stressed you tend to withdraw into yourself, which is not really good for you. A much better strategy would be to verbalise what you are thinking, even though this is not always particularly easy to do.

There are many people in the world who think they know you well, but each and every one of them knows only one Aquarian. There are always more, each a unique individual and probably as much of a mystery to you as they would be to all your relatives and friends, that is if any of them suspected just how deep and mysterious you can be. Despite these facts, your mind is clear and concise, enabling you to get to the truth of any given situation almost immediately. You should never doubt your intuitive foresight and, in the main, must always back your hunches. It is rare indeed for you to be totally wrong about the outcome of any potential situation and your genuine originality of thought is the greatest gift providence has bestowed on you.

Making the best of yourself

Interacting with the world is most important to you. Although you can sometimes be a good deal quieter than the other Air signs of Gemini and Libra, you are still a born communicator, with a great need to live your life to the full. If you feel hemmed in or constrained by circumstances, you are not going to show your best face to family, friends or colleagues. That's why you must move heaven and earth to make certain that you are not tied down in any way. Maintaining a sense of freedom is really just a mental state to Aquarius but it is absolutely vital to your well-being.

As far as work is concerned you need to be doing something that allows you the room you need to move. Any occupation that means thinking on your feet would probably suit you fine. All the same you feel more comfortable in administrative surroundings, rather than getting your hands dirty. Any profession that brings change and variety on a daily basis would be best. You are a good team operator, and yet can easily lead from the front. Don't be frightened to show colleagues that you have an original way of looking at life and that you are an inveterate problem solver.

In terms of friendship you tend to be quite catholic in your choice of pals. Making the best of yourself means keeping things that way. You are not naturally jealous yourself but you do tend to attract friends who are. Make it plain that you can't tie yourself down to any one association, no matter how old or close it may be. At least if you do this nobody can suggest that they weren't warned when you wander off to talk to someone else. Personal relationships are a different matter, though it's hardly likely that you would live in the pocket of your partner. In any situation you need space to breathe, and this includes romantic attachments. People who know you well will not try to hem you in.

Don't be frightened to show your unconventional, even wild side to the world at large. You are a bold character, with a great deal to say and a natural warmth that could melt an iceberg. This is the way providence made you and it is only right to use your gifts to the full.

The impressions you give

You are not a naturally secretive person and don't hold back very much when it comes to speaking your mind. It might be suggested therefore that the external and internal Aquarian is more or less the same person. Although generally true, it has to be remembered that you have a multi-faceted nature and one that adapts quickly to changing circumstances. It is this very adaptability that sets you apart in the eyes of the world.

You often make decisions based on intuitive foresight and although many Aquarians are of above average intelligence, you won't always make use of a deep knowledge of any given situation. In essence you often do what seems right, though you tend to act whilst others are still standing around and thinking. This makes you good to have around in a crisis and convinces many of those looking on that you are incredibly capable, relaxed and confident. Of course this isn't always the case, but even a nervous interior tends to breed outward action in the case of your zodiac sign, so the world can be forgiven for jumping to the wrong conclusion.

People like you – there's no doubt about that. However, you must realise that you have a very upfront attitude, which on occasions is going to get you into trouble. Your occasional weirdness, rather than being a turn-off, is likely to stimulate the interest that the world has in you. Those with whom you come into contact invariably find your personality to be attractive, generous, high-spirited and refreshing. For all these reasons it is very unlikely that you would actually make many enemies, even if some folk are clearly jealous of the easy way you have with the world.

One of the great things about Aquarians is that they love to join in. As a result you may find yourself doing all sorts of things that others would find either difficult or frightening. You can be zany, wild and even mad on occasions, but these tendencies will only get you liked all the more. The world will only tire of you if you allow yourself to get down in the dumps or grumpy – a very rare state for Aquarius.

The way forward

In terms of living your life to the full it is probable that you don't need any real advice from an astrologer. Your confidence allows you to go places that would make some people shiver, whilst your intuitive foresight gives you the armoury you need to deal with a world that can sometimes seem threatening. Yet for all this you are not immune to mental turmoil on occasions, and probably spend rather too much time in the fast lane. It's good to rest, a fact that you need to remember the next time you find yourself surrounded by twenty-seven jobs, all of which you are trying to undertake at the same time.

The more the world turns in the direction of information technology, the happier you are likely to become. If others have difficulty in this age of computers, it's likely that you relish the challenges and the opportunities that these artificial intelligences offer. You are happy with New Age concepts and tend to look at the world with compassion and understanding. Despite the fact that you are always on the go, it's rare for you to be moving forward so fast that you forget either the planet that brought you to birth, or the many underprivileged people who inhabit parts of it. You have a highly developed conscience and tend to work for the good of humanity whenever you can.

You might not be constructed of the highest moral fibre known to humanity, a fact that sometimes shows when it comes to romantic attachments. Many Aquarians play the field at some time in their lives and it's certain that you need a personal relationship that keeps you mentally stimulated. Although your exterior can sometimes seem superficial, you have a deep and sensitive soul – so perhaps you should marry a poet, or at least someone who can cope with the twists and turns of the Aquarian mind. Aquarians who tie themselves down too early, or to the wrong sort of individual, invariable end up regretting the fact.

You can be deeply creative and need to live in clean and cheerful surroundings. Though not exactly a minimalist you don't like clutter and constantly need to spring-clean your home – and your mind. Living with others isn't difficult for you, in fact it's essential. Since you are so adaptable you fit in easily to almost any environment, though you will always ultimately stamp your own character onto it. You love to be loved and offer a great deal in return, even if you are occasionally absent when people need you the most. In essence you are in love with life and so perhaps you should not be too surprised to discover that it is very fond of you too.

AQUARIUS ON THE CUSP

Old Moore is often asked how astrological profiles are altered for those people born at either the beginning or the end of a zodiac sign, or, more properly, on the cusps of a sign. In the case of Aquarius this would be on the 21st of January and for two or three days after, and similarly at the end of the sign, probably from the 17th to the 19th of February. In this year's Astral Diaries, once again, Old Moore sets out to explain the differences regarding cuspid signs.

The Capricorn Cusp – January 21st to 23rd

What really sets you apart is a genuinely practical streak that isn't always present in the sign of Aquarius when taken alone. You are likely to have all the joy of life and much of the devil-may-care attitude of your Sun sign, but at the same time you are capable of getting things done in a very positive way. This makes you likely to achieve a higher degree of material success and means that you ally managerial skills with the potential for rolling up your sleeves and taking part in the 'real work' yourself. Alongside this you are able to harness the naturally intuitive qualities of Aquarius in a very matter-of-fact way. Few people would have the ability to pull the wool over your eyes and you are rarely stuck for a solution, even to apparently difficult problems.

You express yourself less well than Aquarius taken alone, and you may have a sort of reserve that leads others to believe that your mind is full of still waters which run very deep. The air of mystery can actually be quite useful, because it masks an ability to react and move quickly when necessary, which is a great surprise to the people around you. However, there are two sides to every coin and if there is a slightly negative quality to this cuspid position it might lie in the fact that you are not quite the communicator that tends to be the case with Aquarius, and you could go through some fairly quiet and introspective phases that those around you would find somewhat difficult to understand. In a positive sense this offers a fairly wistful aspect to your nature that may, in romantic applications, appear very attractive. There is something deeply magnetic about your nature and it isn't quite possible for everyone to understand what makes you tick. Actually this is part of your appeal because there is nothing like curiosity on the part of others to enhance your profile.

Getting things done is what matters the most to you, harnessed to the ability to see the wider picture in life. It's true that not everyone understands your complex nature, but in friendship you are scarcely short of supportive types. Family members can be especially important to you and personal attachments are invariably made for life.

The Pisces Cusp – February 17th to 19th

It appears that you are more of a thinker than most and achieve depths of contemplation that would be totally alien to some signs of the zodiac. Much of your life is given over to the service you show for humanity as a whole but you don't sink into the depths of despair in the way that some Piscean individuals are inclined to do. You are immensely likeable and rarely stuck for a good idea. You know how to enjoy yourself, even if this quality is usually tied to the support and assistance that you constantly give to those around you.

Many of you will already have chosen a profession that somehow fulfils your need to be of service, and it isn't unusual for Pisces-cusp Aquarians to alter their path in life totally if it isn't fulfilling this most basic requirement. When necessary, you can turn your hand to almost anything, generally giving yourself totally to the task in hand, sometimes to the exclusion of everything else. People with this combination often have two very different sorts of career, sometimes managing to do both at the same time. Confidence in practical matters isn't usually lacking, even if you sometimes think that your thought processes are a little bit muddled.

In love you are ardent and more sincere than Aquarius sometimes seems to be. There can be a tinge of jealousy at work now and again in deep relationships, but you are less likely than Pisces to let this show. You tend to be very protective of the people who are most important in your life and these are probably fewer in number than often seems to be the case for Aquarius. Your love of humanity and the needs it has of you are of supreme importance and you barely let a day pass without offering some sort of assistance. For this reason, and many others, you are a much loved individual and show your most caring face to the world for the majority of your life. Material success can be hard to come by at first, but it isn't really an aspect of life that worries you too much in any case. It is far more important for you to be content with your lot and, if you are happy, it seems that more or less everything else tends to follow.

AQUARIUS AND ITS ASCENDANTS

The nature of every individual on the planet is composed of the rich variety of zodiac signs and planetary positions that were present at the time of their birth. Your Sun sign, which in your case is Aquarius, is one of the many factors when it comes to assessing the unique person you are. Probably the most important consideration, other than your Sun sign, is to establish the zodiac sign that was rising over the eastern horizon at the time that you were born. This is your Ascending or Rising sign. Most popular astrology fails to take account of the Ascendant, and yet its importance remains with you from the very moment of your birth, through every day of your life. The Ascendant is evident in the way you approach the world, and so, when meeting a person for the first time, it is this astrological influence that you are most likely to notice first. Our Ascending sign essentially represents what we appear to be, while the Sun sign is what we feel inside ourselves.

The Ascendant also has the potential for modifying our overall nature. For example, if you were born at a time of day when Aquarius was passing over the eastern horizon (this would be around the time of dawn) then you would be classed as a double Aquarian. As such, you would typify this zodiac sign, both internally and in your dealings with others. However, if your Ascendant sign turned out to be a Fire sign, such as Aries, there would be a profound alteration of nature, away from the expected qualities of Aquarius.

One of the reasons why popular astrology often ignores the Ascendant is that it has always been rather difficult to establish. Old Moore has found a way to make this possible by devising an easy-to-use table, which you will find on page 158 of this book. Using this, you can establish your Ascendant sign at a glance. You will need to know your rough time of birth, then it is simply a case of following the instructions.

For those readers who have no idea of their time of birth it might be worth allowing a good friend, or perhaps your partner, to read through the section that follows this introduction. Someone who deals with you on a regular basis may easily discover your Ascending sign, even though you could have some difficulty establishing it for yourself. A good understanding of this component of your nature is essential if you want to be aware of that 'other person' who is responsible for the way you make contact with the world at large. Your Sun sign, Ascendant sign, and the other pointers in this book will, together, allow you a far better understanding of what makes you tick as an individual. Peeling back the different layers of your astrological make-up can be an enlightening experience, and the Ascendant may represent one of the most important layers of all.

Aquarius with Aquarius Ascendant

You are totally unique and quite original, so much so that very few people could claim to understand what makes you tick. Routines get on your nerves and you need to be out there doing something most of the time. Getting where you want to go in life isn't too difficult, except that when you arrive, your destination might not look half so interesting as it did before. You are well liked and should have many friends. This is not to say that your pals have much in common with each other, because you choose from a wide cross-section of people. Although folks see you as being very reasonable in the main, you are capable of being quite cranky on occasions. Your intuition is extremely strong and is far less likely to let you down than would be the case with some individuals.

Travel is very important to you and you will probably live for some time in a different part of your own country, or even in another part of the world. At work you are more than capable, but do need something to do that you find personally stimulating, because you are not very good at constant routine. You can be relied upon to use your originality and find solutions that are instinctive and brilliant. Most people are very fond of you.

Aquarius with Pisces Ascendant

Here we find the originality of Aquarius balanced by the very sensitive qualities of Pisces, and it makes for a very interesting combination. When it comes to understanding other people you are second to none, but it's certain that you are more instinctive than either Pisces or Aquarius when taken alone. You are better at routines than Aquarius, but also relish a challenge more than the typical Piscean would. Active and enterprising, you tend to know what you want from life, but consideration of others, and the world at large, will always be part of the scenario. People with this combination often work on behalf of humanity and are to be found in social work, the medical profession and religious institutions. As far as beliefs are concerned you don't conform to established patterns, and yet may get closer to the truth of the Creator than many deep theological thinkers have ever been able to do. Acting on impulse as much as you do means that not everyone understands the way your mind works, but your popularity will invariably see you through.

Passionate and deeply sensitive, you are able to negotiate the twists and turns of a romantic life that is hardly likely to be run-of-the-mill. In the end, however, you should be able to discover a very deep personal and spiritual happiness.

Aquarius with Aries Ascendant

If ever anyone could be accused of setting off immediately, but slowly, it has to be you. These are very contradictory signs and the differences will express themselves in a variety of ways. One thing is certain, you have tremendous tenacity and will see a job through patiently from beginning to end, without tiring on the way and ensuring that every detail is taken care of properly. This combination often brings good health and a great capacity for continuity, particularly in terms of the length of life. You are certainly not as argumentative as the typical Aries, but you do know how to get your own way, which is just as well because you are usually thinking on behalf of everyone else and not just on your own account.

At home you can relax, which is a blessing for Aries, though in fact you seldom choose to do so because you always have some project or other on the go. You probably enjoy knocking down and rebuilding walls, though this is a practical tendency and not responsive to relationships, in which you are ardent and sincere. Impetuosity is as close to your heart as is the case for any type of subject, though you certainly have the ability to appear patient and steady. But it's just a front, isn't it?

Aquarius with Taurus Ascendant

There is nothing that you fail to think about deeply and with great intensity. You are wise, honest and very scientific in your approach to life. Routines are necessary in life but you have most of them sorted out well in advance and so always have time to look at the next interesting fact. If you don't spend all your time watching documentaries on the television set, you make a good friend and love to socialise. Most of the great discoveries of the world were probably made by people with this sort of astrological combination, though your nature is rather 'odd' on occasions and so can be rather difficult for others to understand.

You may be most surprised when others tell you that you are eccentric, but you don't really mind too much because for half of the time you are not inhabiting the same world as the rest of us. Because you can be delightfully dotty you are probably much loved and cherished by your friends, of which there are likely to be many. Family members probably adore you too, and you can be guaranteed to entertain anyone with whom you come into contact. The only fly in the ointment is that you sometimes lose track of reality, whatever that might be, and fly high in your own atmosphere of rarefied possibilities.

Aquarius with Gemini Ascendant

If you were around in the 1960s there is every chance that you were the first to go around with flowers in your hair. You are unconventional, original, quirky and entertaining. Few people would fail to notice your presence and you take life as it comes, even though on most occasions you are firmly in the driving seat. It all probability you care very much about the planet on which you live and the people with whom you share it. Not everyone understands you, but that does not really matter, for you have more than enough communication skills to put your message across intact. You should avoid wearing yourself out by worrying about things that you cannot control, and you definitely gain from taking time out to meditate. However, whether or not you allow yourself that luxury remains to be seen.

If you are not the most communicative form of Gemini subject then you must come a close second. Despite this fact much of what you have to say makes real sense and you revel in the company of interesting, intelligent and stimulating people, whose opinions on a host of matters will add to your own considerations. You are a true original in every sense of the word and the mere fact of your presence in the world is bound to add to the enjoyment of life experienced by the many people with whom you make contact.

Aquarius with Cancer Ascendant

The truly original spark, for which the sign of Aquarius is famed, can only enhance the caring qualities of Cancer, and is also inclined to bring the Crab out of its shell to a much greater extent than would be the case with certain other zodiac combinations. Aquarius is a party animal and never arrives without something interesting to say, which is doubly the case when the reservoir of emotion and consideration that is Cancer is feeding the tap. Your nature can be rather confusing for even you to deal with, but you are inspirational, bright, charming and definitely fun to be around.

The Cancer element in your nature means that you care about your home and the people to whom you are related. You are also a good and loyal friend, who would keep attachments for much longer than could be expected for Aquarius alone. You love to travel and can be expected to make many journeys to far-off places during your life. Some attention will have to be paid to your health, because you are capable of burning up masses of nervous energy, often without getting the periods of rest and contemplation that are essential to the deeper qualities of the sign of Cancer. Nevertheless you have determination, resilience and a refreshing attitude that lifts the spirits of the people in your vicinity.

Aquarius with Leo Ascendant

All associations with Aquarius bring originality, and you are no exception. You aspire to do your best most of the time but manage to achieve your objectives in an infinitely amusing and entertaining way. Not that you set out to do so, because if you are an actor on the stage of life, it seems as though you are a natural one. There is nothing remotely pretentious about your breezy personality or your ability to occupy the centre of any stage. This analogy is quite appropriate because you probably like the theatre. Being in any situation when reality is suspended for a while suits you down to the ground, and in any case you may regularly ask yourself if you even recognise what reality is. Always asking questions, both of yourself and the world at large, you soldier on relentlessly, though not to the exclusion of having a good time on the way.

Keeping to tried and tested paths is not your way. You are a natural trailblazer who is full of good ideas and who has the energy to put them into practice. You care deeply for the people who play an important part in your life but are wise enough to allow them the space they need to develop their own personalities along the way. Most people like you, many love you, and one or two think that you really are the best thing since sliced bread.

Aquarius with Virgo Ascendant

How could anyone make the convention unconventional? Well, if anyone can manage, you can. There are great contradictions here, because on the one hand you always want to do the expected thing, but the Aquarian quality within your nature loves to surprise everyone on the way. If you don't always know what you are thinking or doing, it's a pretty safe bet that others won't either, so it's important on occasions really to stop and think. However this is not a pressing concern, because you tend to live a fairly happy life and muddle through no matter what. Other people tend to take to you well and it is likely that you will have many friends. You tend to be bright and cheerful and can approach even difficult tasks with the certainty that you have the skills necessary to see them through to their conclusion. Give and take are important factors in the life of any individual and particularly so in your case. Because you can stretch yourself in order to understand what makes other people think and act in the way that they do, you have the reputation of being a good friend and a reliable colleague.

In love you can be somewhat more fickle than the typical Virgoan, and yet you are always interesting to live with. Where you are, things happen, and you mix a sparkling wit with deep insights.

Aquarius with Libra Ascendant

Stand by for a truly interesting and very inspiring combination here, but one that is sometimes rather difficult to fathom, even for the sort of people who believe themselves to be very perceptive. The reason for this could be that any situation has to be essentially fixed and constant in order to get a handle on it, and this is certainly not the case for the Aquarian–Libran type. The fact is that both these signs are Air signs, and to a certain extent as unpredictable as the wind itself.

To most people you seem to be original, frank, free and very outspoken. Not everything you do makes sense to others and if you were alive during the hippy era, it is likely that you went around with flowers in your hair, for you are a free-thinking idealist at heart. With age you mature somewhat, but never too much, because you will always see the strange, the comical and the original in life. This is what keeps you young and is one of the factors that makes you so very attractive to members of the opposite sex. Many people will want to 'adopt' you and you are at your very best when in company.

Much of your effort is expounded on others and yet, unless you discipline yourself a good deal, personal relationships of the romantic sort can bring certain difficulties. Careful planning is necessary.

Aquarius with Scorpio Ascendant

Here we have a combination that shows much promise and a flexibility that allows many changes in direction, allied to a power to succeed, sometimes very much against all the odds. Aquarius lightens the load of the Scorpio mind, turning the depths into potential, and intuitive foresight into a means for getting on in life. There are depths here, because even airy Aquarius isn't so easy to understand, and it is therefore a fact that some people with this combination will always be something of a mystery. However, even this fact can be turned to your advantage because it means that people will always be looking at you. Confidence is so often the key to success in life and the Scorpio–Aquarius mix offers this, or at least appears to do so. Even when this is not entirely the case, the fact that everyone around you believes it to be true is often enough.

You are usually good to know, and show a keen intellect and a deep intelligence, aided by a fascination for life that knows no bounds. When at your best you are giving, understanding, balanced and active. On those occasions when things are not going well for you, beware of a stubborn streak and the need to be sensational. Keep it light and happy and you won't go far wrong. Most of you are very, very much loved.

Aquarius with Sagittarius Ascendant

There is an original streak to your nature which is very attractive to the people with whom you share your life. Always different, ever on the go and anxious to try out the next experiment in life, you are interested in almost everything, and yet deeply attached to almost nothing. Everyone you know thinks that you are a little 'odd', but you probably don't mind them believing this because you know it to be true. In fact it is possible that you positively relish your eccentricity, which sets you apart from the common herd and means that you are always going to be noticed.

Although it may seem strange with this combination of Air and Fire, you can be distinctly cool on occasions, have a deep and abiding love of your own company now and again and won't be easily understood. Love comes fairly easily to you but there are times when you are accused of being self-possessed, self-indulgent and not willing enough to fall in line with the wishes of those around you. Despite this you walk on and on down your own path. At heart you are an extrovert and you love to party, often late into the night. Luxury appeals to you, though it tends to be of the transient sort. Travel could easily play a major and a very important part in your life.

Aquarius with Capricorn Ascendant

Here the determination of Capricorn is assisted by a slightly more adaptable quality and an off-beat personality that tends to keep everyone else guessing. You don't care to be quite so predictable as the archetypal Capricorn would be, and there is a more idealistic quality here, or at least one that shows more. A greater number of friends than Capricorn usually keeps is likely, though less than the true Aquarian would gather. Few people doubt your sincerity, though by no means all of them understand what makes you tick. Unfortunately you are not in a position to help them out, because you are not too sure yourself. All the same, you muddle through and can be very capable when the mood takes you.

Being a natural traveller, you love to see new places and would be quite fascinated by cultures that are very different to your own. People with this combination are inclined to spend some time living abroad and may even settle there. You look out for the underdog and will always have time for a good cause, no matter what it takes to help. In romantic terms you are a reliable partner, though with a slightly wayward edge which, if anything, tends to make you even more attractive. Listen to your intuition, which is well honed and rarely lets you down. Generally speaking you are very popular.

THE MOON AND THE PART IT PLAYS IN YOUR LIFE

In astrology the Moon is probably the single most important heavenly body after the Sun. Its unique position, as partner to the Earth on its journey around the solar system, means that the Moon appears to pass through the signs of the zodiac extremely quickly. The zodiac position of the Moon at the time of your birth plays a great part in personal character and is especially significant in the build-up of your emotional nature.

Sun Moon Cycles

The first lunar cycle deals with the part the position of the Moon plays relative to your Sun sign. I have made the fluctuations of this pattern easy for you to understand by means of a simple cyclic graph. It appears on the first page of each 'Your Month At A Glance', under the title 'Highs and Lows'. The graph displays the lunar cycle and you will soon learn to understand how its movements have a bearing on your level of energy and your abilities.

Your Own Moon Sign

Discovering the position of the Moon at the time of your birth has always been notoriously difficult because tracking the complex zodiac positions of the Moon is not easy. This process has been reduced to three simple stages with Old Moore's unique Lunar Tables. A breakdown of the Moon's zodiac positions can be found from page 25 onwards, so that once you know what your Moon Sign is, you can see what part this plays in the overall build-up of your personal character.

If you follow the instructions on the next page you will soon be able to work out exactly what zodiac sign the Moon occupied on the day that you were born and you can then go on to compare the reading for this position with those of your Sun sign and your Ascendant. It is partly the comparison between these three important positions that goes towards making you the unique individual you are.

HOW TO DISCOVER YOUR MOON SIGN

This is a three-stage process. You may need a pen and a piece of paper but if you follow the instructions below the process should only take a minute or so.

STAGE 1 First of all you need to know the Moon Age at the time of your birth. If you look at Moon Table 1, on page 23, you will find all the years between 1909 and 2007 down the left side. Find the year of your birth and then trace across to the right to the month of your birth. Where the two intersect you will find a number. This is the date of the New Moon in the month that you were born. You now need to count forward the number of days between the New Moon and your own birthday. For example, if the New Moon in the month of your birth was shown as being the 6th and you were born on the 20th, your Moon Age Day would be 14. If the New Moon in the month of your birth came after your birthday, you need to count forward from the New Moon in the previous month, which, if you were born in January, means you must look at December in the previous year. You cannot count from December in the year of your birth, as that month is *after* your birth. Whatever the result, jot this number down so that you do not forget it.

STAGE 2 Take a look at Moon Table 2 on page 24. Down the left hand column look for the date of your birth. Now trace across to the month of your birth. Where the two meet you will find a letter. Copy this letter down alongside your Moon Age Day.

STAGE 3 Moon Table 3 on page 24 will supply you with the zodiac sign the Moon occupied on the day of your birth. Look for your Moon Age Day down the left hand column and then for the letter you found in Stage 2. Where the two converge you will find a zodiac sign and this is the sign occupied by the Moon on the day that you were born.

Your Zodiac Moon Sign Explained

You will find a profile of all zodiac Moon Signs on pages 25 to 28, showing in yet another way how astrology helps to make you into the individual that you are. In each daily entry of the Astral Diary you can find the zodiac position of the Moon for every day of the year. This also allows you to discover your lunar birthdays. Since the Moon passes through all the signs of the zodiac in about a month, you can expect something like twelve lunar birthdays each year. At these times you are likely to be emotionally steady and able to make the sort of decisions that have real, lasting value.

MOON TABLE 1

YEAR	DEC	JAN	FEB	YEAR	DEC	JAN	FEB	YEAR	DEC	JAN	FEB
1909	12	22	20	1942	8	16	15	1975	3	12	11
1910	1/30	11	9	1943	27	6	4	1976	21	1/31	29
1911	20	29	28	1944	15	25	24	1977	10	19	18
1912	9	18	17	1945	4	14	12	1978	29	9	7
1913	27	7	6	1946	23	3	2	1979	18	27	26
1914	17	25	24	1947	12	21	19	1980	7	16	15
1915	6	15	14	1948	1/30	11	9	1981	26	6	4
1916	25	5	3	1949	19	29	27	1982	15	25	23
1917	13	24	22	1950	9	18	16	1983	4	14	13
1918	2	12	11	1951	28	7	6	1984	22	3	1
1919	21	1/31	–	1952	17	26	25	1985	12	21	19
1920	10	20	19	1953	6	15	14	1986	1/30	10	9
1921	29	9	8	1954	25	5	3	1987	20	29	28
1922	18	27	26	1955	14	24	22	1988	9	19	17
1923	8	17	15	1956	2	13	11	1989	28	7	6
1924	26	6	5	1957	21	1/30	–	1990	17	26	25
1925	15	24	23	1958	10	19	18	1991	6	15	14
1926	5	14	12	1959	29	9	7	1992	24	4	3
1927	24	3	2	1960	18	27	26	1993	14	23	22
1928	12	21	19	1961	7	16	15	1994	2	11	10
1929	1/30	11	9	1962	26	6	5	1995	22	1/30	–
1930	19	29	28	1963	15	25	23	1996	10	20	18
1931	9	18	17	1964	4	14	13	1997	28	9	7
1932	27	7	6	1965	22	3	1	1998	18	27	26
1933	17	25	24	1966	12	21	19	1999	7	17	16
1934	6	15	14	1967	1/30	10	9	2000	26	6	4
1935	25	5	3	1968	20	29	28	2001	15	25	23
1936	13	24	22	1969	9	19	17	2002	4	13	12
1937	2	12	11	1970	28	7	6	2003	23	3	1
1938	21	1/31	–	1971	17	26	25	2004	11	21	20
1939	10	20	19	1972	6	15	14	2005	30	10	9
1940	28	9	8	1973	25	5	4	2006	20	29	28
1941	18	27	26	1974	14	24	22	2007	9	18	16

TABLE 2

MOON TABLE 3

DAY	JAN	FEB
1	A	D
2	A	D
3	A	D
4	A	D
5	A	D
6	A	D
7	A	D
8	A	D
9	A	D
10	A	E
11	B	E
12	B	E
13	B	E
14	B	E
15	B	E
16	B	E
17	B	E
18	B	E
19	B	E
20	B	F
21	C	F
22	C	F
23	C	F
24	C	F
25	C	F
26	C	F
27	C	F
28	C	F
29	C	F
30	C	–
31	D	–

M/D	A	B	C	D	E	F	G
0	CP	AQ	AQ	AQ	PI	PI	PI
1	AQ	AQ	AQ	PI	PI	PI	AR
2	AQ	AQ	PI	PI	PI	AR	AR
3	AQ	PI	PI	PI	AR	AR	AR
4	PI	PI	AR	AR	AR	AR	TA
5	PI	AR	AR	AR	TA	TA	TA
6	AR	AR	AR	TA	TA	TA	GE
7	AR	AR	TA	TA	TA	GE	GE
8	AR	TA	TA	TA	GE	GE	GE
9	TA	TA	GE	GE	GE	CA	CA
10	TA	GE	GE	GE	CA	CA	CA
11	GE	GE	GE	CA	CA	CA	LE
12	GE	GE	CA	CA	CA	LE	LE
13	GE	CA	CA	LE	LE	LE	LE
14	CA	CA	LE	LE	LE	VI	VI
15	CA	LE	LE	LE	VI	VI	VI
16	LE	LE	LE	VI	VI	VI	LI
17	LE	LE	VI	VI	VI	LI	LI
18	LE	VI	VI	VI	LI	LI	LI
19	VI	VI	VI	LI	LI	LI	SC
20	VI	LI	LI	LI	SC	SC	SC
21	LI	LI	LI	SC	SC	SC	SA
22	LI	LI	SC	SC	SC	SA	SA
23	LI	SC	SC	SC	SA	SA	SA
24	SC	SC	SC	SA	SA	SA	CP
25	SC	SA	SA	SA	CP	CP	CP
26	SA	SA	SA	CP	CP	CP	AQ
27	SA	SA	CP	CP	AQ	AQ	AQ
28	SA	CP	CP	AQ	AQ	AQ	AQ
29	CP	CP	CP	AQ	AQ	AQ	PI

AR = Aries, TA = Taurus, GE = Gemini, CA = Cancer, LE = Leo, VI = Virgo, LI = Libra, SC = Scorpio, SA = Sagittarius, CP = Capricorn, AQ = Aquarius, PI = Pisces

MOON SIGNS

Moon in Aries

You have a strong imagination, courage, determination and a desire to do things in your own way and forge your own path through life.

Originality is a key attribute; you are seldom stuck for ideas although your mind is changeable and you could take the time to focus on individual tasks. Often quick-tempered, you take orders from few people and live life at a fast pace. Avoid health problems by taking regular time out for rest and relaxation.

Emotionally, it is important that you talk to those you are closest to and work out your true feelings. Once you discover that people are there to help, there is less necessity for you to do everything yourself.

Moon in Taurus

The Moon in Taurus gives you a courteous and friendly manner, which means you are likely to have many friends.

The good things in life mean a lot to you, as Taurus is an Earth sign that delights in experiences which please the senses. Hence you are probably a lover of good food and drink, which may in turn mean you need to keep an eye on the bathroom scales, especially as looking good is also important to you.

Emotionally you are fairly stable and you stick by your own standards. Taureans do not respond well to change. Intuition also plays an important part in your life.

Moon in Gemini

You have a warm-hearted character, sympathetic and eager to help others. At times reserved, you can also be articulate and chatty: this is part of the paradox of Gemini, which always brings duplicity to the nature. You are interested in current affairs, have a good intellect, and are good company and likely to have many friends. Most of your friends have a high opinion of you and would be ready to defend you should the need arise. However, this is usually unnecessary, as you are quite capable of defending yourself in any verbal confrontation.

Travel is important to your inquisitive mind and you find intellectual stimulus in mixing with people from different cultures. You also gain much from reading, writing and the arts but you do need plenty of rest and relaxation in order to avoid fatigue.

Moon in Cancer

The Moon in Cancer at the time of birth is a fortunate position as Cancer is the Moon's natural home. This means that the qualities of compassion and understanding given by the Moon are especially enhanced in your nature, and you are friendly and sociable and cope well with emotional pressures. You cherish home and family life, and happily do the domestic tasks. Your surroundings are important to you and you hate squalor and filth. You are likely to have a love of music and poetry.

Your basic character, although at times changeable like the Moon itself, depends on symmetry. You aim to make your surroundings comfortable and harmonious, for yourself and those close to you.

Moon in Leo

The best qualities of the Moon and Leo come together to make you warm-hearted, fair, ambitious and self-confident. With good organisational abilities, you invariably rise to a position of responsibility in your chosen career. This is fortunate as you don't enjoy being an 'also-ran' and would rather be an important part of a small organisation than a menial in a large one.

You should be lucky in love, and happy, provided you put in the effort to make a comfortable home for yourself and those close to you. It is likely that you will have a love of pleasure, sport, music and literature. Life brings you many rewards, most of them as a direct result of your own efforts, although you may be luckier than average and ready to make the best of any situation.

Moon in Virgo

You are endowed with good mental abilities and a keen receptive memory, but you are never ostentatious or pretentious. Naturally quite reserved, you still have many friends, especially of the opposite sex. Marital relationships must be discussed carefully and worked at so that they remain harmonious, as personal attachments can be a problem if you do not give them your full attention.

Talented and persevering, you possess artistic qualities and are a good homemaker. Earning your honours through genuine merit, you work long and hard towards your objectives but show little pride in your achievements. Many short journeys will be undertaken in your life.

Moon in Libra

With the Moon in Libra you are naturally popular and make friends easily. People like you, probably more than you realise, you bring fun to a party and are a natural diplomat. For all its good points, Libra is not the most stable of astrological signs and, as a result, your emotions can be a little unstable too. Therefore, although the Moon in Libra is said to be good for love and marriage, your Sun sign and Rising sign will have an important effect on your emotional and loving qualities.

You must remember to relate to others in your decision-making. Co-operation is crucial because Libra represents the 'balance' of life that can only be achieved through harmonious relationships. Conformity is not easy for you because Libra, an Air sign, likes its independence.

Moon in Scorpio

Some people might call you pushy. In fact, all you really want to do is to live life to the full and protect yourself and your family from the pressures of life. Take care to avoid giving the impression of being sarcastic or impulsive and use your energies wisely and constructively.

You have great courage and you invariably achieve your goals by force of personality and sheer effort. You are fond of mystery and are good at predicting the outcome of situations and events. Travel experiences can be beneficial to you.

You may experience problems if you do not take time to examine your motives in a relationship, and also if you allow jealousy, always a feature of Scorpio, to cloud your judgement.

Moon in Sagittarius

The Moon in Sagittarius helps to make you a generous individual with humanitarian qualities and a kind heart. Restlessness may be intrinsic as your mind is seldom still. Perhaps because of this, you have a need for change that could lead you to several major moves during your adult life. You are not afraid to stand your ground when you know your judgement is right, you speak directly and have good intuition.

At work you are quick, efficient and versatile and so you make an ideal employee. You need work to be intellectually demanding and do not enjoy tedious routines.

In relationships, you anger quickly if faced with stupidity or deception, though you are just as quick to forgive and forget. Emotionally, there are times when your heart rules your head.

Moon in Capricorn

The Moon in Capricorn makes you popular and likely to come into the public eye in some way. The watery Moon is not entirely comfortable in the Earth sign of Capricorn and this may lead to some difficulties in the early years of life. An initial lack of creative ability and indecision must be overcome before the true qualities of patience and perseverance inherent in Capricorn can show through. .

You have good administrative ability and are a capable worker, and if you are careful you can accumulate wealth. But you must be cautious and take professional advice in partnerships, as you are open to deception. You may be interested in social or welfare work, which suit your organisational skills and sympathy for others.

Moon in Aquarius

The Moon in Aquarius makes you an active and agreeable person with a friendly, easy-going nature. Sympathetic to the needs of others, you flourish in a laid-back atmosphere. You are broad-minded, fair and open to suggestion, although sometimes you have an unconventional quality which others can find hard to understand.

You are interested in the strange and curious, and in old articles and places. You enjoy trips to these places and gain much from them. Political, scientific and educational work interests you and you might choose a career in science or technology.

Money-wise, you make gains through innovation and concentration and Lunar Aquarians often tackle more than one job at a time. In love you are kind and honest.

Moon in Pisces

You have a kind, sympathetic nature, somewhat retiring at times, but you always take account of others' feelings and help when you can.

Personal relationships may be problematic, but as life goes on you can learn from your experiences and develop a better understanding of yourself and the world around you.

You have a fondness for travel, appreciate beauty and harmony and hate disorder and strife. You may be fond of literature and would make a good writer or speaker yourself. You have a creative imagination and may come across as an incurable romantic. You have strong intuition, maybe bordering on a mediumistic quality, which sets you apart from the mass. You may not be rich in cash terms, but your personal gifts are worth more than gold.

AQUARIUS IN LOVE

Discover how compatible in love you are with people from the same and other signs of the zodiac. Five stars equals a match made in heaven!

Aquarius meets Aquarius

This is a good match for several reasons. Most importantly, although it sounds arrogant, Aquarians like themselves. At its best, Aquarius is one of the fairest, most caring and genuinely pleasant zodiac signs and so it is only when faced by the difficulties created by others that it shows a less favourable side. Put two Aquarians together and voilà – instant success! Personal and family life should bring more joy. On the whole, a platform for adventure based on solid foundations. Star rating: *****

Aquarius meets Pisces

Zodiac signs that follow each other often have something in common, but this is not the case with Aquarius and Pisces. Both signs are deeply caring, but in different ways. Pisces is one of the deepest zodiac signs, and Aquarius simply isn't prepared to embark on the journey. Pisceans, meanwhile, would probably find Aquarians superficial and even flippant. On the positive side there is potential for a well-balanced relationship, but unless one party is untypical of their zodiac sign, it often doesn't get started. Star rating: **

Aquarius meets Aries

Aquarius is an Air sign, and Air and Fire often work well together, but not in the case of Aries and Aquarius. The average Aquarian lives in what the Ram sees as a fantasy world, so a meeting of minds is unlikely. Of course, the dominant side of Aries could be trained by the devil-may-care attitude of Aquarius. There are meeting points but they are difficult to establish. However, given sufficient time and an open mind on both sides, a degree of happiness is possible. Star rating: **

Aquarius meets Taurus

In any relationship of which Aquarius is a part, surprises abound. It is difficult for Taurus to understand the soul-searching, adventurous, changeable Aquarian, but on the positive side, the Bull is adaptable and can respond well to a dose of excitement. Aquarians are kind and react well to the same quality coming back at them. Both are friendly, capable of deep affection and basically creative. Unfortunately, Taurus simply doesn't know what makes Aquarius tick, which could lead to feelings of isolation, even if these don't always show on the surface. Star rating: **

Aquarius meets Gemini

Aquarius is commonly mistaken for a Water sign, but in fact it's ruled by the Air element, and this is the key to its compatibility with Gemini. Both signs mix freely socially, and each has an insatiable curiosity. There is plenty of action, lots of love, but very little rest, and so great potential for success if they don't wear each other out! Aquarius revels in its own eccentricity, and encourages Gemini to emulate this. Theirs will be an unconventional household, but almost everyone warms to this crazy and unpredictable couple. Star rating: *****

Aquarius meets Cancer

Cancer is often attracted to Aquarius and, as Aquarius is automatically on the side of anyone who fancies it, so there is the potential for something good here. Cancer loves Aquarius' devil-may-care approach to life, but also recognises and seeks to strengthen the basic lack of self-confidence that all Air signs try so hard to keep secret. Both signs are natural travellers and are quite adventurous. Their family life could be unusual, but friends would recognise a caring, sharing household with many different interests shared by people genuinely in love. Star rating: ***

Aquarius meets Leo

The problem here is that Aquarius doesn't think in the general sense of the word, it knows. Leo, on the other hand, is more practical and relies more on logical reasoning, and consequently it doesn't understand Aquarius very well. Aquarians can also appear slightly frosty in their appreciation of others and this, too, will annoy Leo. This is a good match for a business partnership because Aquarius is astute, while Leo is brave, but personally the prognosis is less promising. Tolerance, understanding and forbearance are all needed to make this work. Star rating: **

Aquarius meets Virgo

Aquarius is a strange sign because no matter how well one knows it, it always manages to surprise. For this reason, against the odds, it's quite likely that Aquarius will form a sucessful relationship with Virgo. Aquarius is changeable, unpredictable and often quite odd, while Virgo is steady, a fuss-pot and very practical. Herein lies the key. What one sign needs, the other provides and that may be the surest recipe for success imaginable. On-lookers may not know why the couple are happy, but they will recognise that this is the case. Star rating: ****

Aquarius meets Libra

One of the best combinations imaginable, partly because both are Air signs and so share a common meeting point. But perhaps the more crucial factor is that both signs respect each other. Aquarius loves life and originality, and is quite intellectual. Libra is similar, but more balanced and rather less eccentric. A visit to this couple's house would be entertaining and full of zany wit, activity and excitement. Both are keen to travel and may prefer to 'find themselves' before taking on too many domestic responsibilities. Star rating: *****

Aquarius meets Scorpio

This is a promising and practical combination. Scorpio responds well to Aquarius' persistent exploration of its deep nature and so this generally shy sign becomes lighter, brighter and more inspirational. Meanwhile, Aquarians are rarely as sure of themselves as they like to appear and are reassured by Scorpio's constant, steady and determined support. Both signs want to be kind to each other, which is a good starting point to a relationship that should be warm most of the time and extremely hot occasionally. Star rating: ****

Aquarius meets Sagittarius

Both Sagittarius and Aquarius are into mind games, which may lead to something of an intellectual competition. If one side is happy to be 'bamboozled' it won't be a problem, but it is more likely that the relationship will turn into a competition, which won't auger well for its long-term future. However, on the plus side, both signs are adventurous and sociable, so as long as there is always something new and interesting to do, the match could turn out very well. Star rating: **

Aquarius meets Capricorn

Probably one of the least likely combinations, as Capricorn and Aquarius are unlikely to choose each other in the first place, unless one side is quite untypical of their sign. Capricorn approaches things in a practical way and likes to get things done, while Aquarius works almost exclusively for the moment and relies heavily on intuition. Their attitudes to romance are also diametrically opposed: Aquarius' moods tend to swing from red hot to ice cold in a minute, which is alien to steady Capricorn. Star rating: **

VENUS:
THE PLANET OF LOVE

If you look up at the sky around sunset or sunrise you will often see Venus in close attendance to the Sun. It is arguably one of the most beautiful sights of all and there is little wonder that historically it became associated with the goddess of love. But although Venus does play an important part in the way you view love and in the way others see you romantically, this is only one of the spheres of influence that it enjoys in your overall character.

Venus has a part to play in the more cultured side of your life and has much to do with your appreciation of art, literature, music and general creativity. Even the way you look is responsive to the part of the zodiac that Venus occupied at the start of your life, though this fact is also down to your Sun sign and Ascending sign. If, at the time you were born, Venus occupied one of the more gregarious zodiac signs, you will be more likely to wear your heart on your sleeve, as well as to be more attracted to entertainment, social gatherings and good company. If on the other hand Venus occupied a quiet zodiac sign at the time of your birth, you would tend to be more retiring and less willing to shine in public situations.

It's good to know what part the planet Venus plays in your life for it can have a great bearing on the way you appear to the rest of the world and since we all have to mix with others, you can learn to make the very best of what Venus has to offer you.

One of the great complications in the past has always been trying to establish exactly what zodiac position Venus enjoyed when you were born because the planet is notoriously difficult to track. However, I have solved that problem by creating a table that is exclusive to your Sun sign, which you will find on the following page.

Establishing your Venus sign could not be easier. Just look up the year of your birth on the page opposite and you will see a sign of the zodiac. This was the sign that Venus occupied in the period covered by your sign in that year. If Venus occupied more than one sign during the period, this is indicated by the date on which the sign changed, and the name of the new sign. For instance, if you were born in 1945, Venus was in Pisces until the 12th February, after which time it was in Aries. If you were born before 12th February your Venus sign is Pisces, if you were born on or after 12th February, your Venus sign is Aries. Once you have established the position of Venus at the time of your birth, you can then look in the pages which follow to see how this has a bearing on your life as a whole.

1909 CAPRICORN / 9.2 AQUARIUS
1910 AQUARIUS
1911 AQUARIUS / 3.2 PISCES
1912 SAGITTARIUS /
   30.1 CAPRICORN
1913 PISCES / 16.2 ARIES
1914 CAPRICORN / 26.1 AQUARIUS /
   19.2 PISCES
1915 SAGITTARIUS / 7.2 CAPRICORN
1916 PISCES / 14.2 ARIES
1917 CAPRICORN / 9.2 AQUARIUS
1918 AQUARIUS
1919 AQUARIUS / 3.2 PISCES
1920 SAGITTARIUS /
   30.1 CAPRICORN
1921 PISCES / 15.2 ARIES
1922 CAPRICORN / 25.1 AQUARIUS /
   18.2 PISCES
1923 SAGITTARIUS / 7.2 CAPRICORN
1924 PISCES / 13.2 ARIES
1925 CAPRICORN / 9.2 AQUARIUS
1926 AQUARIUS
1927 AQUARIUS / 2.2 PISCES
1928 SAGITTARIUS /
   29.1 CAPRICORN
1929 PISCES / 14.2 ARIES
1930 CAPRICORN / 25.1 AQUARIUS /
   18.2 PISCES
1931 SAGITTARIUS / 6.2 CAPRICORN
1932 PISCES / 13.2 ARIES
1933 CAPRICORN / 8.2 AQUARIUS
1934 AQUARIUS
1935 AQUARIUS / 2.2 PISCES
1936 SAGITTARIUS /
   29.1 CAPRICORN
1937 PISCES / 13.2 ARIES
1938 CAPRICORN / 24.1 AQUARIUS /
   17.2 PISCES
1939 SAGITTARIUS / 6.2 CAPRICORN
1940 PISCES / 12.2 ARIES
1941 CAPRICORN / 8.2 AQUARIUS
1942 AQUARIUS
1943 AQUARIUS / 1.2 PISCES
1944 SAGITTARIUS /
   28.1 CAPRICORN
1945 PISCES / 12.2 ARIES
1946 CAPRICORN / 24.1 AQUARIUS /
   17.2 PISCES
1947 SAGITTARIUS / 6.2 CAPRICORN
1948 PISCES / 12.2 ARIES
1949 CAPRICORN / 7.2 AQUARIUS
1950 AQUARIUS
1951 AQUARIUS / 1.2 PISCES
1952 SAGITTARIUS /
   27.1 CAPRICORN
1953 PISCES / 11.2 ARIES
1954 CAPRICORN / 23.1 AQUARIUS /
   16.2 PISCES
1955 SAGITTARIUS / 6.2 CAPRICORN
1956 PISCES / 11.2 ARIES
1957 CAPRICORN / 7.2 AQUARIUS

1958 AQUARIUS
1959 AQUARIUS / 31.1 PISCES
1960 SAGITTARIUS /
   27.1 CAPRICORN
1961 PISCES / 9.2 ARIES
1962 CAPRICORN / 23.1 AQUARIUS /
   15.2 PISCES
1963 SAGITTARIUS / 6.2 CAPRICORN
1964 PISCES / 11.2 ARIES
1965 CAPRICORN / 6.2 AQUARIUS
1966 AQUARIUS
1967 AQUARIUS / 30.1 PISCES
1968 SAGITTARIUS /
   26.1 CAPRICORN
1969 PISCES / 7.2 ARIES
1970 CAPRICORN / 22.1 AQUARIUS /
   15.2 PISCES
1971 SAGITTARIUS / 5.2 CAPRICORN
1972 PISCES / 10.2 ARIES
1973 CAPRICORN / 5.2 AQUARIUS
1974 AQUARIUS / 7.2 CAPRICORN
1975 AQUARIUS / 30.1 PISCES
1976 SAGITTARIUS /
   26.1 CAPRICORN
1977 PISCES / 5.2 ARIES
1978 CAPRICORN / 22.1 AQUARIUS /
   14.2 PISCES
1979 SAGITTARIUS / 5.2 CAPRICORN
1980 PISCES / 10.2 ARIES
1981 CAPRICORN / 5.2 AQUARIUS
1982 AQUARIUS / 29.1 CAPRICORN
1983 AQUARIUS / 29.1 PISCES
1984 SAGITTARIUS /
   25.1 CAPRICORN
1985 PISCES / 5.2 ARIES
1986 AQUARIUS / 14.2 PISCES
1987 SAGITTARIUS / 5.2 CAPRICORN
1988 PISCES / 9.2 ARIES
1989 CAPRICORN / 4.2 AQUARIUS
1990 AQUARIUS / 23.1 CAPRICORN
1991 AQUARIUS / 29.1 PISCES
1992 SAGITTARIUS /
   25.1 CAPRICORN
1993 PISCES / 4.2 ARIES
1994 AQUARIUS / 13.2 PISCES
1995 SAGITTARIUS / 5.2 CAPRICORN
1996 PISCES / 9.2 ARIES
1997 CAPRICORN / 4.2 AQUARIUS
1998 AQUARIUS / 23.1 CAPRICORN
1999 AQUARIUS / 29.1 PISCES
2000 SAGITTARIUS /
   25.1 CAPRICORN
2001 PISCES / 4.2 ARIES
2002 AQUARIUS / 13.2 PISCES
2003 SAGITTARIUS
2004 PISCES / 9.2 AQUARIUS
2005 CAPRICORN / 6.2 AQUARIUS
2006 AQUARIUS / 14.1 CAPRICORN
2007 AQUARIUS / 29.1 PISCES

VENUS THROUGH THE ZODIAC SIGNS

Venus in Aries

Amongst other things, the position of Venus in Aries indicates a fondness for travel, music and all creative pursuits. Your nature tends to be affectionate and you would try not to create confusion or difficulty for others if it could be avoided. Many people with this planetary position have a great love of the theatre, and mental stimulation is of the greatest importance. Early romantic attachments are common with Venus in Aries, so it is very important to establish a genuine sense of romantic continuity. Early marriage is not recommended, especially if it is based on sympathy. You may give your heart a little too readily on occasions.

Venus in Taurus

You are capable of very deep feelings and your emotions tend to last for a very long time. This makes you a trusting partner and lover, whose constancy is second to none. In life you are precise and careful and always try to do things the right way. Although this means an ordered life, which you are comfortable with, it can also lead you to be rather too fussy for your own good. Despite your pleasant nature, you are very fixed in your opinions and quite able to speak your mind. Others are attracted to you and historical astrologers always quoted this position of Venus as being very fortunate in terms of marriage. However, if you find yourself involved in a failed relationship, it could take you a long time to trust again.

Venus in Gemini

As with all associations related to Gemini, you tend to be quite versatile, anxious for change and intelligent in your dealings with the world at large. You may gain money from more than one source but you are equally good at spending it. There is an inference here that you are a good communicator, via either the written or the spoken word, and you love to be in the company of interesting people. Always on the look-out for culture, you may also be very fond of music, and love to indulge the curious and cultured side of your nature. In romance you tend to have more than one relationship and could find yourself associated with someone who has previously been a friend or even a distant relative.

Venus in Cancer

You often stay close to home because you are very fond of family and enjoy many of your most treasured moments when you are with those you love. Being naturally sympathetic, you will always do anything you can to support those around you, even people you hardly know at all. This charitable side of your nature is your most noticeable trait and is one of the reasons why others are naturally so fond of you. Being receptive and in some cases even psychic, you can see through to the soul of most of those with whom you come into contact. You may not commence too many romantic attachments but when you do give your heart, it tends to be unconditionally.

Venus in Leo

It must become quickly obvious to almost anyone you meet that you are kind, sympathetic and yet determined enough to stand up for anyone or anything that is truly important to you. Bright and sunny, you warm the world with your natural enthusiasm and would rarely do anything to hurt those around you, or at least not intentionally. In romance you are ardent and sincere, though some may find your style just a little overpowering. Gains come through your contacts with other people and this could be especially true with regard to romance, for love and money often come hand in hand for those who were born with Venus in Leo. People claim to understand you, though you are more complex than you seem.

Venus in Virgo

Your nature could well be fairly quiet no matter what your Sun sign might be, though this fact often manifests itself as an inner peace and would not prevent you from being basically sociable. Some delays and even the odd disappointment in love cannot be ruled out with this planetary position, though it's a fact that you will usually find the happiness you look for in the end. Catapulting yourself into romantic entanglements that you know to be rather ill-advised is not sensible, and it would be better to wait before you committed yourself exclusively to any one person. It is the essence of your nature to serve the world at large and through doing so it is possible that you will attract money at some stage in your life.

Venus in Libra

Venus is very comfortable in Libra and bestows upon those people who have this planetary position a particular sort of kindness that is easy to recognise. This is a very good position for all sorts of friendships and also for romantic attachments that usually bring much joy into your life. Few individuals with Venus in Libra would avoid marriage and since you are capable of great depths of love, it is likely that you will find a contented personal life. You like to mix with people of integrity and intelligence but don't take kindly to scruffy surroundings or work that means getting your hands too dirty. Careful speculation, good business dealings and money through marriage all seem fairly likely.

Venus in Scorpio

You are quite open and tend to spend money quite freely, even on those occasions when you don't have very much. Although your intentions are always good, there are times when you get yourself in to the odd scrape and this can be particularly true when it comes to romance, which you may come to late or from a rather unexpected direction. Certainly you have the power to be happy and to make others contented on the way, but you find the odd stumbling block on your journey through life and it could seem that you have to work harder than those around you. As a result of this, you gain a much deeper understanding of the true value of personal happiness than many people ever do, and are likely to achieve true contentment in the end.

Venus in Sagittarius

You are lighthearted, cheerful and always able to see the funny side of any situation. These facts enhance your popularity, which is especially high with members of the opposite sex. You should never have to look too far to find romantic interest in your life, though it is just possible that you might be too willing to commit yourself before you are certain that the person in question is right for you. Part of the problem here extends to other areas of life too. The fact is that you like variety in everything and so can tire of situations that fail to offer it. All the same, if you choose wisely and learn to understand your restless side, then great happiness can be yours.

Venus in Capricorn

The most notable trait that comes from Venus in this position is that it makes you trustworthy and able to take on all sorts of responsibilities in life. People are instinctively fond of you and love you all the more because you are always ready to help those who are in any form of need. Social and business popularity can be yours and there is a magnetic quality to your nature that is particularly attractive in a romantic sense. Anyone who wants a partner for a lover, a spouse and a good friend too would almost certainly look in your direction. Constancy is the hallmark of your nature and unfaithfulness would go right against the grain. You might sometimes be a little too trusting.

Venus in Aquarius

This location of Venus offers a fondness for travel and a desire to try out something new at every possible opportunity. You are extremely easy to get along with and tend to have many friends from varied backgrounds, classes and inclinations. You like to live a distinct sort of life and gain a great deal from moving about, both in a career sense and with regard to your home. It is not out of the question that you could form a romantic attachment to someone who comes from far away or be attracted to a person of a distinctly artistic and original nature. What you cannot stand is jealousy, for you have friends of both sexes and would want to keep things that way.

Venus in Pisces

The first thing people tend to notice about you is your wonderful, warm smile. Being very charitable by nature you will do anything to help others, even if you don't know them well. Much of your life may be spent sorting out situations for other people, but it is very important to feel that you are living for yourself too. In the main, you remain cheerful, and tend to be quite attractive to members of the opposite sex. Where romantic attachments are concerned, you could be drawn to people who are significantly older or younger than yourself or to someone with a unique career or point of view. It might be best for you to avoid marrying whilst you are still very young.

THE ASTRAL DIARY
HOW THE DIAGRAMS WORK

Through the picture diagrams in the Astral Diary I want to help you to plot your year. With them you can see where the positive and negative aspects will be found in each month. To make the most of them, all you have to do is remember where and when!

Let me show you how they work …

THE MONTH AT A GLANCE

Just as there are twelve separate zodiac signs, so astrologers believe that each sign has twelve separate aspects to life. Each of the twelve segments relates to a different personal aspect. I list them all every month so that their meanings are always clear.

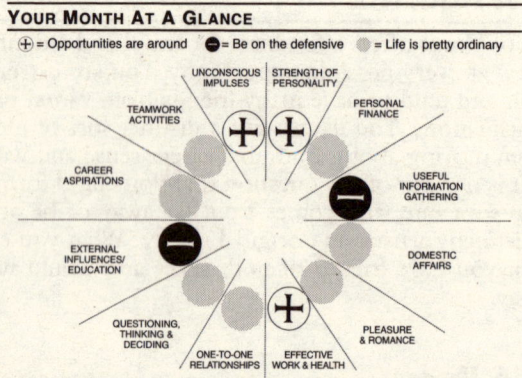

YOUR MONTH AT A GLANCE

⊕ = Opportunities are around   ● = Be on the defensive   ● = Life is pretty ordinary

- UNCONSCIOUS IMPULSES
- STRENGTH OF PERSONALITY
- PERSONAL FINANCE
- TEAMWORK ACTIVITIES
- CAREER ASPIRATIONS
- USEFUL INFORMATION GATHERING
- EXTERNAL INFLUENCES/ EDUCATION
- DOMESTIC AFFAIRS
- QUESTIONING, THINKING & DECIDING
- PLEASURE & ROMANCE
- ONE-TO-ONE RELATIONSHIPS
- EFFECTIVE WORK & HEALTH

I have designed this chart to show you how and when these twelve different aspects are being influenced throughout the year. When there is a shaded circle, nothing out of the ordinary is to be expected. However, when a circle turns white with a plus sign, the influence is positive. Where the circle is black with a minus sign, it is a negative.

YOUR ENERGY RHYTHM CHART

On the opposite page is a picture diagram in which I am linking your zodiac group to the rhythm of the Moon. In doing this I have calculated when you will be gaining strength from its influence and equally when you may be weakened by it.

If you think of yourself as being like the tides of the ocean then you may understand how your own energies must also rise and fall. And if you understand how it works and when it is working, then you can better organise your activities to achieve more and get things done more easily.

YOUR ENERGY RHYTHM CHART

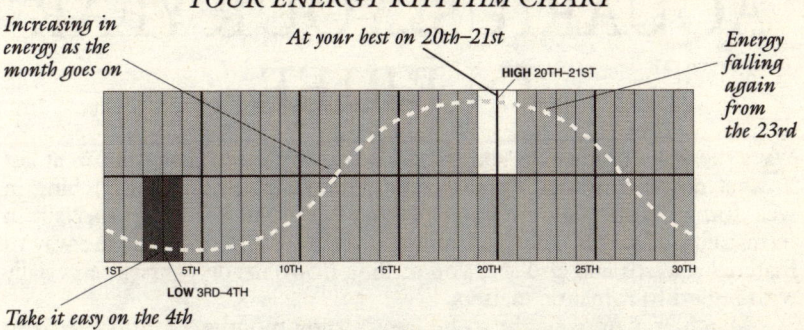

Increasing in energy as the month goes on

At your best on 20th–21st

Energy falling again from the 23rd

HIGH 20TH–21ST

1ST 5TH 10TH 15TH 20TH 25TH 30TH

LOW 3RD–4TH

Take it easy on the 4th

MOVING PICTURE SCREEN
Love, money, career and vitality measured every week

The diagram at the end of each week is designed to be informative and fun. The arrows move up and down the scale to give you an idea of the strength of your opportunities in each area. If LOVE stands at plus 4, then get out and put yourself about because things are going your way in romance! The further down the arrow goes, the weaker the opportunities. Do note that the diagram is an overall view of your astrological aspects and therefore reflects a trend which may not concur with every day in that cycle.

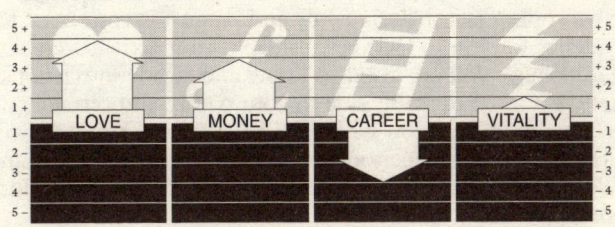

5 +				+ 5
4 +				+ 4
3 +				+ 3
2 +				+ 2
1 +	LOVE	MONEY	CAREER	VITALITY	+ 1

AND FINALLY:

am . . . .

pm . . . .

The two lines that are left blank in each daily entry of the Astral Diary are for your own personal use. You may find them ideal for keeping a check on birthdays or appointments, though it could be an idea to make notes from the astrological trends and diagrams a few weeks in advance. Some of the lines are marked with a key, which indicates the working of astrological cycles in your life. Look out for them each week as they are the best days to take action or make decisions. The daily text tells you which area of your life to focus on.

☿ = Mercury is retrograde on that day.

AQUARIUS: YOUR YEAR IN BRIEF

As the year commences you should be quite pleased that you can at last get down to something concrete. The planets show you pitching in well during January and probably making significant headway, especially in terms of your career. February ought to bring a little more in the way of material rewards and also sees you settling down inside yourself, especially with regard to romantic matters.

March and April ought to be fairly steady months for Aquarius. You won't have quite the same zest you did at the start of the year but you are steady in your approach and still making significant progress. There are better trends about when it comes to impressing others and you seem to be everyone's cup of tea. What friends and colleagues think about you is probably very important at this time and you will be deliberately playing to the gallery much of the time.

With the arrival of the summer months, May and June will find you active, enterprising, still popular with others and in a perfect position to feather your nest in a financial sense. This is a time during which you think up new strategies and then put them into action. New starts in love for some Aquarians are more than likely, and emotions run quite deep.

The overriding factor during July and August is your need for change and a tendency for you to feel very restless if your activities are curtailed in any way. Although you are good to know and steady in relationships, you can also show a more excitable side to your nature and certainly won't take kindly to anyone telling you what you have to do. You need to exercise some patience during this period and will also be travelling about as much as possible. Any long distance journeys are likely to take place during these two months.

As the summer starts to draw to its close September and October bring some different trends. It is clear that many Aquarians will now become more sentimental, slightly less pushy and somewhat inclined to withdraw into themselves from time to time. You show yourself to be extremely generous, especially with friends and family members, and you also seem to have more time for your own interests.

At the close of the year, November and December bring indications of another big push. After having withdrawn somewhat from the rat race during the autumn, you are now back in the running and anxious to get ahead. You might not always be certain of yourself but you are willing to take a chance and that's part of being an Aquarian. The Christmas period should be warm and settled, even if you sometimes get itchy feet when things become rather too staid and sentimental.

January

2007

YOUR MONTH AT A GLANCE

⊕ = Opportunities are around   ⊖ = Be on the defensive   ⬤ = Life is pretty ordinary

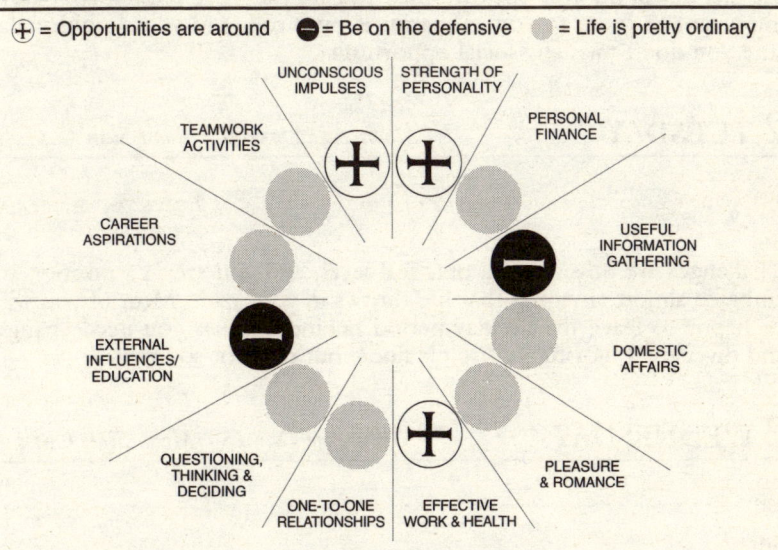

JANUARY HIGHS AND LOWS

Here I show you how the rhythms of the Moon will affect you this month. Like the tide, your energies and abilities will rise and fall with its pattern. When it is above the centre line, go for it, when it is below, you should be resting.

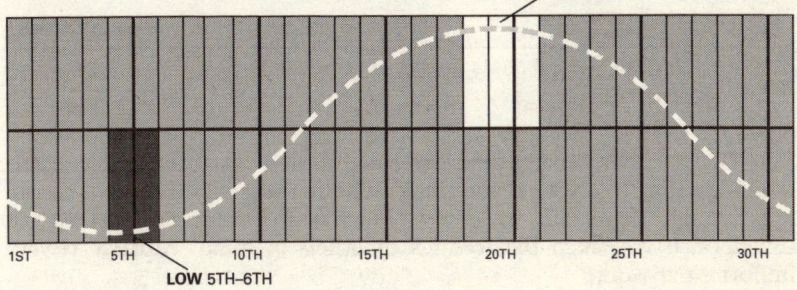

1 MONDAY
Moon Age Day 13   Moon Sign Gemini

am . . . .

pm . . . .
This is a time to be making social plans of one sort or another. You have
scope to put your luck to the test as far as love is concerned and to make
the first day of the year one on which you are willing to tell someone how
important they are to you. Aquarius is on a roll, and you should make
sure you don't miss any social opportunity.

2 TUESDAY
Moon Age Day 14   Moon Sign Gemini

am . . . .

pm . . . .
Challenges are possible at a practical level, and you are in a position to
embrace almost anything that life throws in your path. Most of you will
be happy to leave the holiday period behind because you need change
and diversity. Enjoying yourself is fine – but only for so long!

3 WEDNESDAY
Moon Age Day 15   Moon Sign Cancer

am . . . .

pm . . . .
Don't be afraid to take the odd chance today, especially at work. You are
capable and have great determination, something you can ensure that
others recognise. Action is the name of the game and you won't take no
for an answer in situations you understand well. Trends suggest some
physical restlessness today.

4 THURSDAY
Moon Age Day 16   Moon Sign Cancer

am . . . .

pm . . . .
You have the ability to get others to listen to what you have to say, so this
is an ideal time to say what you think. Whether you will be quite as tactful
as you might be remains to be seen, but you do have some diplomacy to
call upon if you keep the feelings of others in mind. Attitude is very
important at work.

5 FRIDAY
Moon Age Day 17   Moon Sign Leo

am . . . .

pm . . . .
Genuine progress could be slowed significantly today. The Moon has entered Leo, which is your opposite zodiac sign. This brings the period that crops up each month and which is known as the lunar low. Your best approach is to keep your expectations to a minimum and don't push your luck in a financial sense.

6 SATURDAY
Moon Age Day 18   Moon Sign Leo

am . . . .

pm . . . .
Any headway you feel you have made so far this year may now seem less certain. This has more to do with your attitude than it does with reality, so beware of reacting too strongly. You may decide to rely on family members and friends to take some of the decisions at the start of this weekend, though by tomorrow you can get back on form.

7 SUNDAY
Moon Age Day 19   Moon Sign Virgo

am . . . .

pm . . . .
Deep discussions, particularly with loved ones, are probably best avoided at the moment. Your mind is now working at a fairly superficial level and you should enjoy the cut and thrust of social activities. Friends may be less of a problem than relatives at the moment.

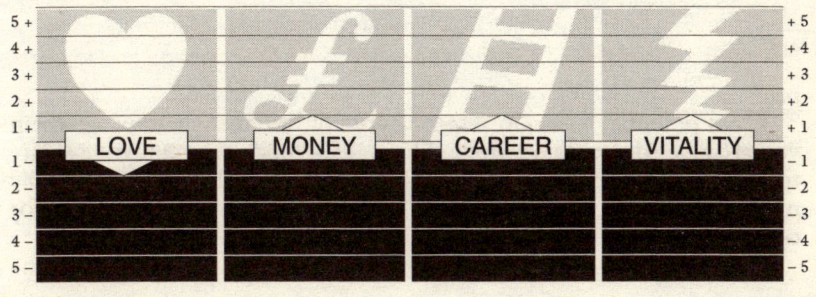

8 MONDAY

Moon Age Day 20   Moon Sign Virgo

am . . . .

pm . . . .
Venus is now in your solar third house, encouraging you to focus on love.
It shouldn't be hard to find the right words to sweep almost anyone off
their feet, but you could land yourself in some hot water if you are doing
it too much. In a more practical sense you may decide to delegate some
responsibilities today.

9 TUESDAY

Moon Age Day 21   Moon Sign Virgo

am . . . .

pm . . . .
You have what it takes to get the best from social situations today and to
show the very gregarious side of your Aquarian nature. Not everyone you
meet will be equally helpful, but you also have what it takes to talk
awkward types round to your point of view. Your charming persona
remains intact under current influences.

10 WEDNESDAY

Moon Age Day 22   Moon Sign Libra

am . . . .

pm . . . .
You can make progress in your professional life today and show the world
what Aquarius is like when fully in gear. Even if you are expected to take
on extra responsibilities, this shouldn't bother you at all. People from the
past could be making return visits to your life around now.

11 THURSDAY

Moon Age Day 23   Moon Sign Libra

am . . . .

pm . . . .
This has potential to be an inspiring sort of day and one during which
you are able to get masses done. Once again much relies on your ability
to communicate, and you have what it takes to turn heads when it really
matters. There are likely to be small financial gains on offer, and plans for
others in the near future.

12 FRIDAY

Moon Age Day 24   Moon Sign Scorpio

am . . . .

pm . . . .
Mars is now in your solar first house, and this is part of what is encouraging you to be so vital and alive. The only slight fly in the ointment is that you might not be quite so patient as is usually the case. This is especially true when you are dealing with those who seem to work hard at being stupid.

13 SATURDAY

Moon Age Day 25   Moon Sign Scorpio

am . . . .

pm . . . .
Friendship issues and group encounters are well accented, and you could be quite gregarious in a social sense. This is not the sort of weekend that lends itself to concentrating too much on practical issues, and the very best scenario would be to spend time away from home doing something exciting.

14 SUNDAY

Moon Age Day 26   Moon Sign Scorpio

am . . . .

pm . . . .
A confident gesture on your part could help you to attract the attention of others. This is no time to hide your light under a bushel and you really do need to shine when in any sort of company. You might be called upon to do something you haven't tried before, but nerves are hardly likely to get in the way.

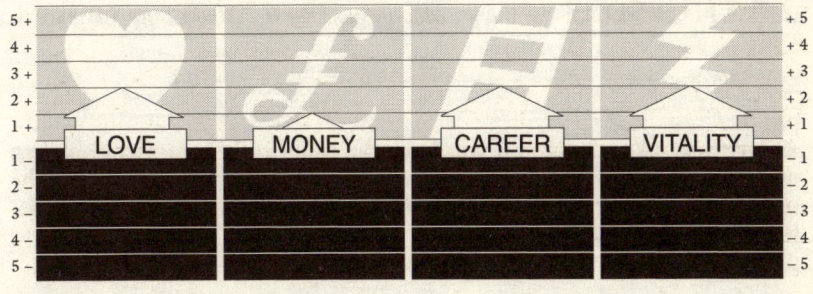

15 MONDAY   *Moon Age Day 27   Moon Sign Sagittarius*

am . . . .

pm . . . .
Look out for new information that may be available at the start of a new working week. Even if people rely heavily on you, you should be fine when put under any sort of pressure. The attitude of a loved one might take some thinking about and some effort is necessary when it comes to remaining calm in the face of provocation.

16 TUESDAY   *Moon Age Day 28   Moon Sign Sagittarius*

am . . . .

pm . . . .
Getting others to carry out your instructions shouldn't be too difficult, as long as you explain yourself carefully. The fact is that you would probably rather do things yourself, simply because it's quicker. However, there are times when you simply have to delegate, and that is the way things are likely to be right now.

17 WEDNESDAY   *Moon Age Day 29   Moon Sign Capricorn*

am . . . .

pm . . . .
A quieter Aquarius can be put on display now. The Moon has moved into your solar twelfth house and this encourages you to be more contemplative and inclined to spend time thinking about things. This phase only lasts a couple of days, and then you can get yourself right back on form.

18 THURSDAY   *Moon Age Day 0   Moon Sign Capricorn*

am . . . .

pm . . . .
A day to stand and watch if you have the chance. By tomorrow you can make the most of busier trends, but the lull today does give you the opportunity to catch your breath. Others may be relying on you quite heavily and you won't want to let them down. In situations you find personally testing, try to rely on your intuition.

19 FRIDAY
Moon Age Day 1   Moon Sign Aquarius

am . . . .

pm . . . .

Major initiatives now get the green light as you enter that period during which the Moon occupies your own zodiac sign of Aquarius. This is a monthly interlude known as the lunar high and it offers you the best incentive for success. There might be more money about, or at least the chance to set out to make some.

20 SATURDAY
Moon Age Day 2   Moon Sign Aquarius

am . . . .

pm . . . .

When it comes to new initiatives you have all the get-up-and-go you could possibly need. Routines are for the birds now as you sally forth without any detailed plan and work things out as you go. This is Aquarius at its best, and it would be very surprising if you failed to gain some admirers at the moment.

21 SUNDAY
Moon Age Day 3   Moon Sign Aquarius

am . . . .

pm . . . .

For the third day in a row the Moon occupies your zodiac sign and brings with it the potential for a generally good day. If you are not at work during the weekend you will have scope to find ways to have fun and there are likely to be plenty of possibilities around. Why not leave jobs that have to be done at home until another day?

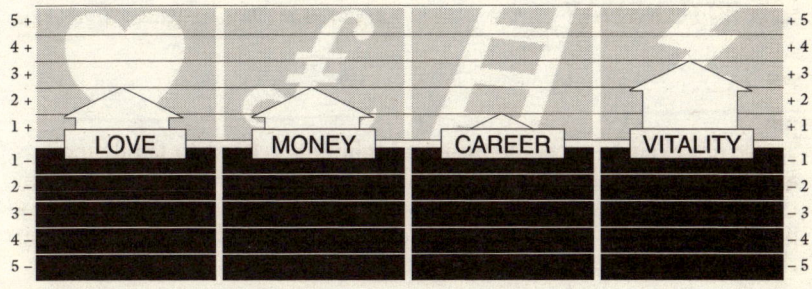

22 MONDAY

Moon Age Day 4   Moon Sign Pisces

am . . . .

pm . . . .
Things should settle down a little and that is probably no bad thing. You
have a tremendous capacity for wearing yourself out like all Air signs, of
which you are one, and you then tend to collapse in a heap. You can best
avoid this today by taking life more steadily in the first place and by
letting others take some of the strain.

23 TUESDAY

Moon Age Day 5   Moon Sign Pisces

am . . . .

pm . . . .
Even if confidence is high and you are still getting a great deal done, you
might be fretting over money. Look at the situation carefully and you
could discover that things are nowhere near as sticky as they might look.
The time is right to get on side with colleagues who you also count as
good friends.

24 WEDNESDAY

Moon Age Day 6   Moon Sign Aries

am . . . .

pm . . . .
Finance and practical matters remain highlighted. Trends assist you to be
slightly more settled in your attitude and to get yourself in the good
books of those who are in a position to offer genuine assistance. You may
decide to spend more time with family members who have got
themselves into a muddle.

25 THURSDAY

Moon Age Day 7   Moon Sign Aries

am . . . .

pm . . . .
There are likely to be some positive highlights related to family matters,
and you have what it takes to move mountains for others. This means
there may be less time to address issues that are important to you
personally, but you are very practically minded and should be able to
think up new schemes as you go along.

26 FRIDAY   *Moon Age Day 8   Moon Sign Taurus*

am . . . .

pm . . . .
Your ego is potentially strong at the moment, but it can also be easily dented. You would be well advised to avoid getting into any sort of row and need to be quite careful when involved in deep discussions. These could easily turn into pointless arguments, which will benefit nobody.

27 SATURDAY   *Moon Age Day 9   Moon Sign Taurus*

am . . . .

pm . . . .
Better financial developments are there for the taking, even if some of them are a little difficult to spot right now. Creative potential is also well starred, and there is an opportunity for you to find things to do around the house that will make both you and other family members more comfortable in the longer term.

28 SUNDAY   *Moon Age Day 10   Moon Sign Gemini*

am . . . .

pm . . . .
Social and leisure pursuits could well demand more from you than you realise. This might be especially true as far as your purse or wallet is concerned. If you use a little thought you can think up things to do that hardly cost you anything at all. What is more, you can make sure these are more enjoyable than any expensive adventure.

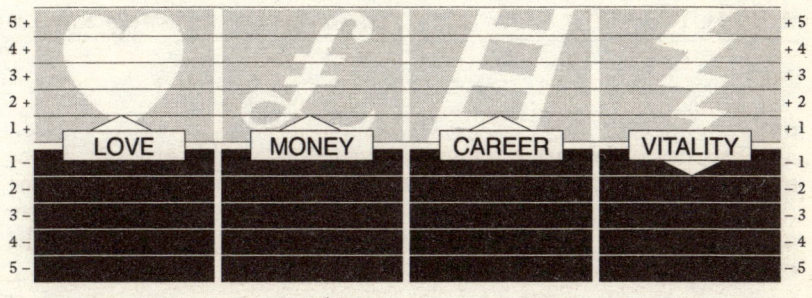

29 MONDAY · *Moon Age Day 11   Moon Sign Gemini*

am . . . .

pm . . . .
Trends highlight your organising skills, which should be useful if you are busy, and not able to give as much attention to certain matters as you might wish. Beware of getting involved in disputes that have nothing at all to do with you, and settle for a quieter day in terms of interactions with others.

30 TUESDAY · *Moon Age Day 12   Moon Sign Cancer*

am . . . .

pm . . . .
You can still be pretty much on form, but there are quieter times coming later in the week so you would be well advised to get as much done today and tomorrow as proves to be possible. It's worth keeping in touch with friends who are at a distance and paying attention to communications that are coming at you from all directions.

31 WEDNESDAY *Moon Age Day 13   Moon Sign Cancer*

am . . . .

pm . . . .
It's possible for you to achieve successes right now that you definitely didn't expect. These are not likely to be regarding major issues, and you could also find that you are winding down somewhat later on. By the evening your best approach is simply to watch and wait, rather than to take part.

1 THURSDAY *Moon Age Day 14   Moon Sign Leo*

am . . . .

pm . . . .
The first day of February brings the lunar low, so this may not be the most inspiring period you have experienced so far this year. All the same there are possible gains to be made. These come as a result of a quieter nature and a more contemplative attitude. Trying to push yourself at the moment could be counter-productive.

2 FRIDAY
Moon Age Day 15   Moon Sign Leo

am . . . .

pm . . . .
Opportunities to make gains in life seem to be few and far between for now, which is why you can turn your mind to the future. Planning, both for the short and medium term, would be a good way to deal with the lunar low, and offers you the chance to retreat from life, whilst at the same time achieving something.

3 SATURDAY
Moon Age Day 16   Moon Sign Leo

am . . . .

pm . . . .
The weekend starts with the Moon still in Leo, though not for very long. You could fight shy of pushing yourself in the morning and may decide that breakfast in bed is the best way forward. It shouldn't take you long to gain speed again, and once you do there are all sorts of social possibilities in the offing.

4 SUNDAY
Moon Age Day 17   Moon Sign Virgo

am . . . .

pm . . . .
Recent efforts begin to show fortunate results. Some of these may have been a little slow in showing themselves, but you can definitely increase the pace of life, and will need to keep your wits about you if you want to make the most of everything that is on offer. Don't forget about the needs of family members and your partner.

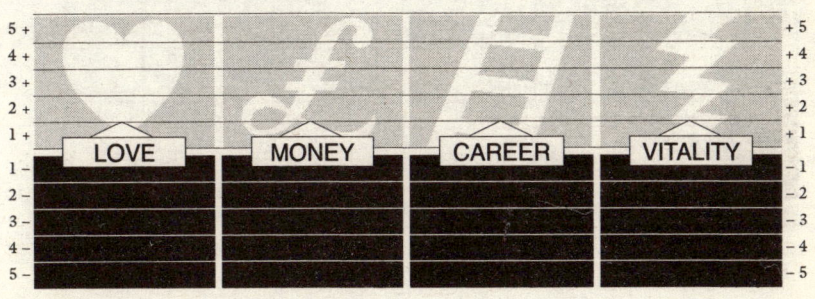

February 2007

YOUR MONTH AT A GLANCE

⊕ = Opportunities are around   ⊖ = Be on the defensive   ⬤ = Life is pretty ordinary

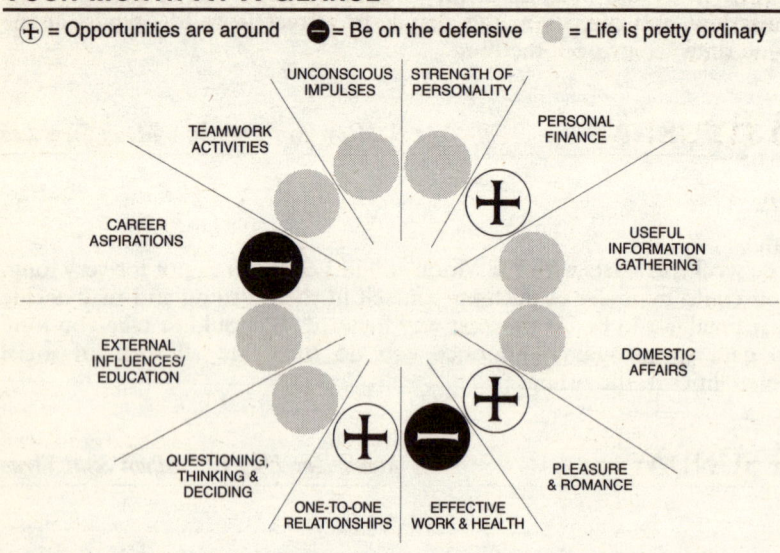

UNCONSCIOUS IMPULSES

STRENGTH OF PERSONALITY

PERSONAL FINANCE

TEAMWORK ACTIVITIES

CAREER ASPIRATIONS

USEFUL INFORMATION GATHERING

EXTERNAL INFLUENCES/ EDUCATION

DOMESTIC AFFAIRS

QUESTIONING, THINKING & DECIDING

ONE-TO-ONE RELATIONSHIPS

EFFECTIVE WORK & HEALTH

PLEASURE & ROMANCE

FEBRUARY HIGHS AND LOWS

Here I show you how the rhythms of the Moon will affect you this month. Like the tide, your energies and abilities will rise and fall with its pattern. When it is above the centre line, go for it, when it is below, you should be resting.

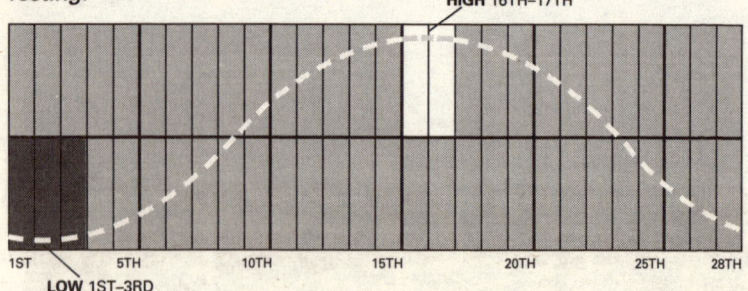

HIGH 16TH–17TH

1ST   5TH   10TH   15TH   20TH   25TH   28TH

LOW 1ST–3RD

5 MONDAY   *Moon Age Day 18   Moon Sign Virgo*

am . . . .

pm . . . .
You may well start the week filled with a desire for new experiences.
There is plenty to be done and you should remain very practical in your
approach to life. Dealing with quieter people could prove to be
something of a problem, but you have what it takes to bring almost
anyone out of their shell.

6 TUESDAY   *Moon Age Day 19   Moon Sign Virgo*

am . . . .

pm . . . .
Trends indicate that friends bring out the best in you, and offer you
scope to get yourself involved in co-operative ventures at this stage of the
week. When it comes to taking decisions, slow and steady wins the race,
even if a part of your mind is urging you onward at a much faster rate.

7 WEDNESDAY   *Moon Age Day 20   Moon Sign Libra*

am . . . .

pm . . . .
You can turn professional matters to your advantage at the moment and
should be quite happy to look at new possibilities that could mean a
change in responsibilities. Try to stay cool, calm and collected, even on
those occasions when there is some provocation about. Routines are
probably necessary, if somewhat tedious.

8 THURSDAY   *Moon Age Day 21   Moon Sign Libra*

am . . . .

pm . . . .
Major initiatives and money-making schemes are around, but whether or
not you decide to become involved in them today depends mainly on
your overall attitude. The social trends are strong and you may decide
that it would be better to dump some of the practical needs of the day in
favour of having fun.

9 FRIDAY
Moon Age Day 22   Moon Sign Scorpio

am . . . .

pm . . . .
Be prepared to apply yourself slightly more than might have been the case yesterday. You may not be so keen to have a good time, but you should remain charming in your attitude and more than able to bring others round to your point of view. Spending more time with family members would be no bad thing.

10 SATURDAY
Moon Age Day 23   Moon Sign Scorpio

am . . . .

pm . . . .
Mercury is now in your solar fourth house, encouraging a willingness to defend family members if you feel they are getting a raw deal. That's fine, but don't go over the top. Even before you fly off the handle you would be wise to make sure that the details you are being given are the correct ones.

11 SUNDAY
Moon Age Day 24   Moon Sign Scorpio

am . . . .

pm . . . .
This is a time of strong intellectual insights and a period during which you may be more likely to respond to gut reactions rather than to simply common sense. When a little bell rings at the back of your mind, it is time to pay attention. There could be some slight financial gains available, and today has potential to be generally rewarding.

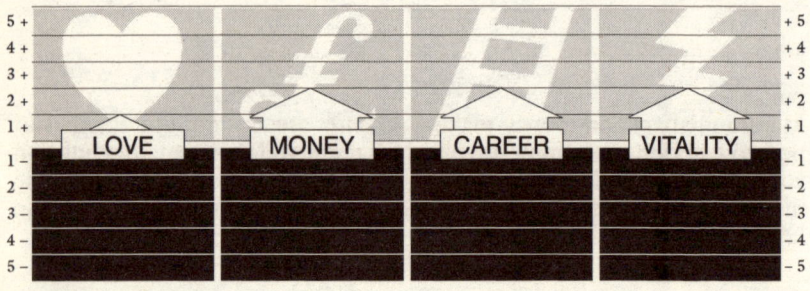

12 MONDAY   *Moon Age Day 25   Moon Sign Sagittarius*

am . . . .

pm . . . .
It's worth getting some peace and quiet if you can for at least part of today. This may be a forlorn wish because it seems that the whole world and his dog has need of you at some stage during the day. By the evening you might be happy to collapse in a heap – but bear in mind that even that desire could be thwarted!

13 TUESDAY   *Moon Age Day 26   Moon Sign Sagittarius*

am . . . .

pm . . . .
Venus joins Mars in your solar fourth house, suggesting that your main concern right now will be for those to whom you are related, either by choice or family ties. Romance is to the fore, but there could be quite a lot of reactions going on and a very steamy period is possible.

14 WEDNESDAY ☿ *Moon Age Day 27   Moon Sign Capricorn*

am . . . .

pm . . . .
Things quieten down just a little as the Moon enters your solar twelfth house. For the next couple of days you may be less impulsive and could show a greater desire to retreat into yourself. Instead of doing exactly what is expected of you, there is a possibility you will take more time out to think of implications.

15 THURSDAY ☿ *Moon Age Day 28   Moon Sign Capricorn*

am . . . .

pm . . . .
You have what it takes to remain essentially steady in your attitude and to be less impulsive than sometimes turns out to be the case for the average Aquarian. This situation could change markedly tomorrow, so make the most of the quieter period and get to know certain people better as a result of your penetrating insights.

16 FRIDAY ☿ *Moon Age Day 0   Moon Sign Aquarius*

am . . . .

pm . . . .
Put your best foot forward today because the Moon has moved into Aquarius, bringing the lunar high for the month and offering much in the way of adventure. It isn't only those things you have planned that matter today. On the contrary, you can definitely afford to act and react instinctively under present trends.

17 SATURDAY ☿ *Moon Age Day 1   Moon Sign Aquarius*

am . . . .

pm . . . .
There is little that is beyond you now that your energies have reached a definite peak. Now is the time to give yourself wholeheartedly to any project that captivates your imagination, whilst at the same time pushing for changes that you know are going to benefit you not only now but also in the medium and long term.

18 SUNDAY ☿ *Moon Age Day 2   Moon Sign Pisces*

am . . . .

pm . . . .
Mars has now moved out of your solar first house. This can help you to take the 'edge' out of your nature and begin to show a kinder and warmer face to the world at large. Where there have been disagreements, you can now bring peace and should be prepared to back down rather than to force almost any issue.

	LOVE	MONEY	CAREER	VITALITY
5 +				+ 5
4 +				+ 4
3 +				+ 3
2 +				+ 2
1 +				+ 1
1 −				− 1
2 −				− 2
3 −				− 3
4 −				− 4
5 −				− 5

19 MONDAY ☿ *Moon Age Day 3   Moon Sign Pisces*

am . . . .

pm . . . .
The best thing you can do today is to get busy. Everything points to an
active and enterprising time and you have what it takes to turn heads.
Don't be in the least surprised today to discover that you have an admirer
and don't even be astonished if you find out that there is more than one!

20 TUESDAY ☿ *Moon Age Day 4   Moon Sign Aries*

am . . . .

pm . . . .
Make family matters lively and rewarding, though issues related to
domestic finances are best left alone for the next couple of days. You
should show your nearest and dearest that you know how to have fun and
that you are considerate of their needs too. Relatives can be friends as
well, and you need to show that this is the case.

21 WEDNESDAY ☿ *Moon Age Day 5   Moon Sign Aries*

am . . . .

pm . . . .
Now you can make the most of more confidence than might have been
the case earlier in the month. Actually there is probably very little change
– it's just a matter of your own attitude. One thing is certain: when you
have to make decisions of any sort today you need not hang around
jumping from foot to foot.

22 THURSDAY ☿ *Moon Age Day 6   Moon Sign Taurus*

am . . . .

pm . . . .
You should have great self-assurance today and a desire to get things
right first time. Not everyone may be in the same frame of mind, and if
you have any difficulty at all it might be in persuading others to follow
your lead. Friends could prove to be very important, and practical
matters are not your only considerations today.

23 FRIDAY ☿ *Moon Age Day 7   Moon Sign Taurus*

am . . . .

pm . . . .
With Venus still strong in your solar fourth house, it's worth showing
concern for those at home, and you can afford to be especially warm
towards your romantic partner. If you don't have one at the moment this
might be as good a time as any to make a play for someone you find to
be especially attractive.

24 SATURDAY ☿ *Moon Age Day 8   Moon Sign Gemini*

am . . . .

pm . . . .
In terms of work you could well be in the midst of a rather busy phase
and this tends to apply whether you work at the weekend or not. When
you are not actually involved in your career you will probably be thinking
about it, but you should also take some time to yourself and enjoy social
possibilities with friends.

25 SUNDAY ☿ *Moon Age Day 9   Moon Sign Gemini*

am . . . .

pm . . . .
Beneficial trends at home remain the major focus for the moment. If you
have had changes or improvements to your home on your mind, this is a
good time to get them started. What may not impress you right now will
be other people's rules and regulations, and you could well react strongly
if pushed.

	5 +				+ 5
4 +				+ 4
3 +				+ 3
2 +				+ 2
1 +				+ 1
LOVE	MONEY	CAREER	VITALITY
1 −				− 1
2 −				− 2
3 −				− 3
4 −				− 4
5 −				− 5

26 MONDAY ☿ *Moon Age Day 10   Moon Sign Gemini*

am . . . .

pm . . . .
Beware of taking too much for granted today. You would be well advised to check and double-check all details, and this is especially important when it comes to travel of any sort. You could enjoy getting away from things at this time and have scope to be much inspired intellectually by almost any change of scene.

27 TUESDAY ☿ *Moon Age Day 11   Moon Sign Cancer*

am . . . .

pm . . . .
There are new gains to be made simply by being the in the right place. If you don't know where that might be, just keep your eyes open. You could also do worse than to listen to what other people are saying. Even casual gossip could allow you to glean some interesting information that you can turn to your advantage.

28 WEDNESDAY ☿ *Moon Age Day 12   Moon Sign Cancer*

am . . . .

pm . . . .
You now have great power to change things, even if you do so in small increments. Even if you are neither pushy nor argumentative, you can still get your own way most of the time. Beware of small mishaps later in the day as the Moon draws close to your opposite sign of Leo.

1 THURSDAY ☿ *Moon Age Day 13   Moon Sign Leo*

am . . . .

pm . . . .
The lunar low coincides with the first day of March, so you may not be on top form to greet the new month. Why not allow others to make some of the running, whilst you sit back and watch for once? Someone you don't see too often could be making a new appearance in your life, and they could bring interesting possibilities.

2 FRIDAY ☿ *Moon Age Day 14 Moon Sign Leo*

am . . . .

pm . . . .
Even if you are still not on top form, this short interlude does at least offer you the chance to look at things more fully and with greater concentration. For now your best approach is to do one job at once, which would certainly be a departure for Aquarius. Friends could show how very warm they can be.

3 SATURDAY ☿ *Moon Age Day 15 Moon Sign Virgo*

am . . . .

pm . . . .
Some quite interesting news could be on offer this weekend, and you could be whisked out of your usual routines by the invitations coming in from other people. Don't worry too much about domestic chores because you can catch up with them later. The time is right to stimulate your mind in some way – that's often number one for Aquarius.

4 SUNDAY ☿ *Moon Age Day 16 Moon Sign Virgo*

am . . . .

pm . . . .
You have the ability to keep on the go today and to show you have recovered from the lunar low. Although this is a Sunday you might be behaving as if it were the middle of a busy week, and might not slacken the pace until you climb into bed. You love to be busy, and have plenty of zest available at the moment.

	LOVE	MONEY	CAREER	VITALITY	
5 +					+ 5
4 +					+ 4
3 +					+ 3
2 +					+ 2
1 +					+ 1
1 –					– 1
2 –					– 2
3 –					– 3
4 –					– 4
5 –					– 5

March 2007

YOUR MONTH AT A GLANCE

+ = Opportunities are around   − = Be on the defensive   ● = Life is pretty ordinary

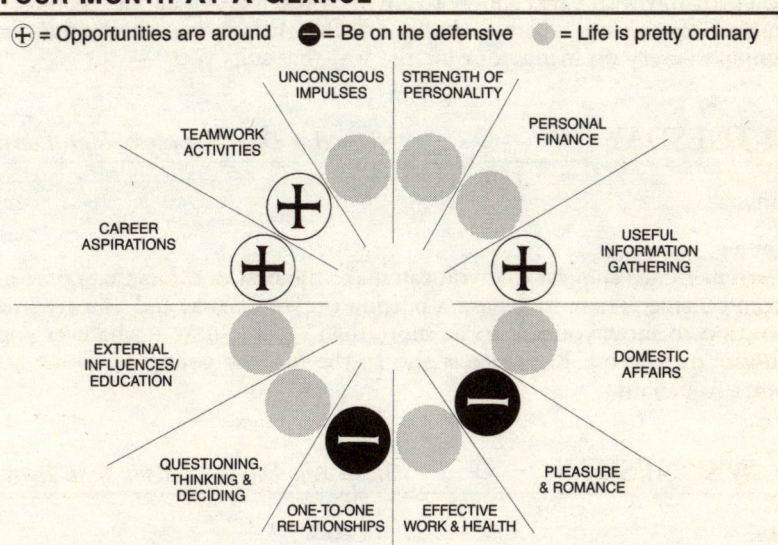

- UNCONSCIOUS IMPULSES
- STRENGTH OF PERSONALITY
- TEAMWORK ACTIVITIES
- PERSONAL FINANCE
- CAREER ASPIRATIONS
- USEFUL INFORMATION GATHERING
- EXTERNAL INFLUENCES/EDUCATION
- DOMESTIC AFFAIRS
- QUESTIONING, THINKING & DECIDING
- ONE-TO-ONE RELATIONSHIPS
- EFFECTIVE WORK & HEALTH
- PLEASURE & ROMANCE

MARCH HIGHS AND LOWS

Here I show you how the rhythms of the Moon will affect you this month. Like the tide, your energies and abilities will rise and fall with its pattern. When it is above the centre line, go for it, when it is below, you should be resting.

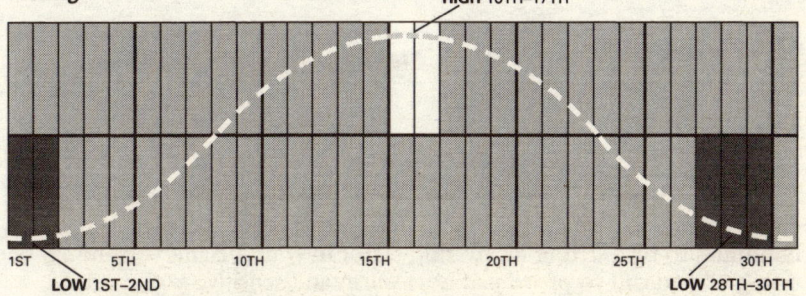

HIGH 16TH–17TH

1ST   5TH   10TH   15TH   20TH   25TH   30TH

LOW 1ST–2ND

LOW 28TH–30TH

61

5 MONDAY ☿ *Moon Age Day 17   Moon Sign Virgo*

am . . . .

pm . . . .
You can afford to work very hard this week, but not because other people expect you to do so. Aquarius is entering a very determined stage and you probably won't take kindly to anyone ordering you about. However, instead of reacting, which is simply a waste of time, your best option is simply to carry on living your life the way that suits you.

6 TUESDAY ☿ *Moon Age Day 18   Moon Sign Libra*

am . . . .

pm . . . .
Current trends suggest that you can make the best of offers that come in from outside. These may have a bearing on your work, and you are in a position to show yourself to be more than capable now – whatever you choose to take on. Romance is also to the fore for young or young-at-heart Aquarians.

7 WEDNESDAY ☿ *Moon Age Day 19   Moon Sign Libra*

am . . . .

pm . . . .
You have what it takes to keep up a brisk general pace to life, which after all is the way you like things to be. Less restrained by the actions or opinions of others, you can push forward mainly under your own steam. There may be moments you need help, but there is just a danger you will be too proud to ask for it.

8 THURSDAY ☿ *Moon Age Day 20   Moon Sign Scorpio*

am . . . .

pm . . . .
You show yourself to be at your very best now when in the company of close friends or when you are alone with your partner. Romance continues to be a strong motivating factor in your life and you should be doing all you can to prove just how warm and sensitive you can be.

9 FRIDAY

Moon Age Day 21   Moon Sign Scorpio

am . . . .

pm . . . .
When it comes to attracting money you have potential now to be in a better position than has been the case for a number of weeks. It isn't so much what you do right now that matters but rather the effort you have put in previously. Be careful though, because cash could well run through your hands like water at the moment.

10 SATURDAY

Moon Age Day 22   Moon Sign Scorpio

am . . . .

pm . . . .
Your capacity for clear-sightedness now sets you apart in the estimation of others, which is why you might feel like an agony aunt before the end of the day. It is unlikely that you will complain much, because it is good to know that people trust you and that they think you have the answers they need.

11 SUNDAY

Moon Age Day 23   Moon Sign Sagittarius

am . . . .

pm . . . .
Your mind is very sharp, enabling ideas to flow well for you at the moment. Active and enterprising, you also have what it takes to strengthen your finances. At the same time you have to remember that this is a Sunday and that you owe some responsibility to the people you don't spend as much time with during the week as you might.

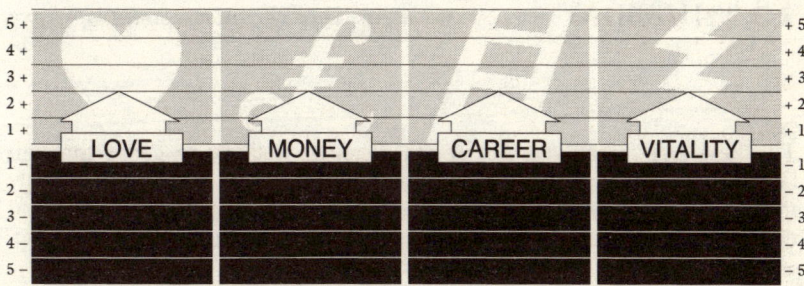

12 MONDAY   *Moon Age Day 24   Moon Sign Sagittarius*

am . . . .

pm . . . .
You needn't be in too much of a hurry to complete practical matters today. It would be best if you took your time, not because you are lacking in energy, though this might be an issue tomorrow. For the moment there is simply the possibility that you might make mistakes through being in a rush.

13 TUESDAY   *Moon Age Day 25   Moon Sign Capricorn*

am . . . .

pm . . . .
For the next three days Aquarius is encouraged to show a much quieter face to the world. There needn't be any loss of effectiveness, and your general level of luck remains essentially good. It is simply that the Moon is now in your solar twelfth house and that could make you less inclined to push your ideas forward.

14 WEDNESDAY   *Moon Age Day 26   Moon Sign Capricorn*

am . . . .

pm . . . .
There are signs that routines might suit you fairly well for much of the time today, and that you will be happy in your own little world for much of the time. The advice you can offer to others should be considered and sensible, and you have what it takes to be especially sensitive to the needs of your partner and those of family members.

15 THURSDAY   *Moon Age Day 27   Moon Sign Capricorn*

am . . . .

pm . . . .
The best enjoyment you get at the moment is likely to come through family life rather than your work. This trend could reverse quickly tomorrow, so make the most of a generally smooth path and a life that doesn't make quite as many demands on you as would usually be the case.

16 FRIDAY
Moon Age Day 28   Moon Sign Aquarius

am . . . .

pm . . . .
You should easily be able to spot opportunities almost instantly today, and the lunar high helps you to pep things up no end. With everything to play for in the financial and career stakes you can make progress towards what you want most of the time and can look ahead well too. When it comes to romance, strike whilst the iron is hot.

17 SATURDAY
Moon Age Day 29   Moon Sign Aquarius

am . . . .

pm . . . .
This is a day during which you are able to call the shots and you needn't ease up as far as the pressure is concerned until you go to bed again. It might seem as if this would be something of a trial, but you clearly have the ability to respond well to pressure and even to soak it up like a sponge at the moment.

18 SUNDAY
Moon Age Day 0   Moon Sign Pisces

am . . . .

pm . . . .
Your strength lies in attracting people right now and in mixing with individuals who have what it takes to move your life forward in some way. There are some gains to be made in the practical sphere of life, but as this is a Sunday you may decide to spend some time with family members and in particular with your romantic partner.

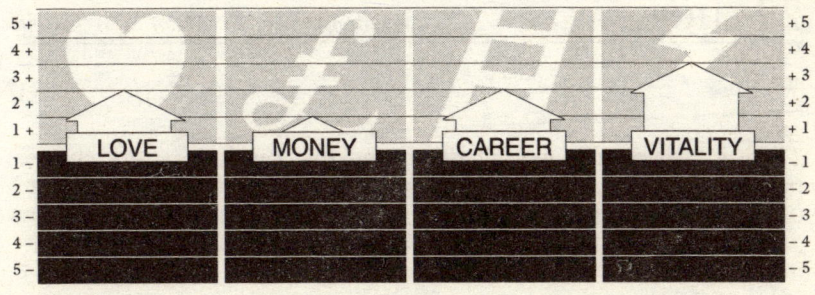

19 MONDAY
Moon Age Day 1   Moon Sign Pisces

am . . . .

pm . . . .
This is a day to look forward to situations that make you look on the
brighter side of life. For those of you who work, this is going to be a week
that offers much of what you need in order to be content. Meanwhile,
you have scope to keep family members happy and to sort out the mess
some of them are getting into.

20 TUESDAY
Moon Age Day 2   Moon Sign Aries

am . . . .

pm . . . .
Mars is in your solar third house now and that could motivate you to be
quite outspoken. With other trends also in operation this may show itself
as a tendency to support others and to fight for the rights of those you
see as being oppressed in some way. A socially-minded Aquarian can now
be put on display.

21 WEDNESDAY
Moon Age Day 3   Moon Sign Aries

am . . . .

pm . . . .
Even if you are still spending a good deal of your time working hard, you
are also in a position to change things to your advantage at home. It
could have occurred to you that the year is growing older and the days
are getting longer. There could be significant incentives around to alter
your home surroundings as spring arrives.

22 THURSDAY
Moon Age Day 4   Moon Sign Taurus

am . . . .

pm . . . .
There is a favourable new phase around that can have a very positive
bearing on leisure and romantic matters. Aquarians who are not involved
in any specific personal attachment at the moment may well be able to
pursue a new relationship. Those who have partners have an opportunity
to make personal moments more interesting.

23 FRIDAY

Moon Age Day 5   Moon Sign Taurus

am . . . .

pm . . . .
Family trends still look very good and there are small rewards available, possibly of a financial nature and as a result of moves you made in the past. You could be just a little nostalgic on occasions, and whilst there is no real harm in this you would do well to remind yourself that there is no future in the past.

24 SATURDAY

Moon Age Day 6   Moon Sign Gemini

am . . . .

pm . . . .
The positive trends continue, though this could turn out to be a day on which you decide to retire from some of the responsibilities you shoulder during the week. Leisure pursuits could well be very physical in nature and some of you might be embarking on a new health kick. If so, you would be wise to take it steady at first.

25 SUNDAY

Moon Age Day 7   Moon Sign Gemini

am . . . .

pm . . . .
Variety and warmth in equal quantities could enable you to make this day somewhat special. Beware of getting too involved with matters that have nothing to do with you and curb that curiosity if you don't want to get bogged down in someone else's mire. There is enough to do today keeping yourself tuned in to what lies ahead.

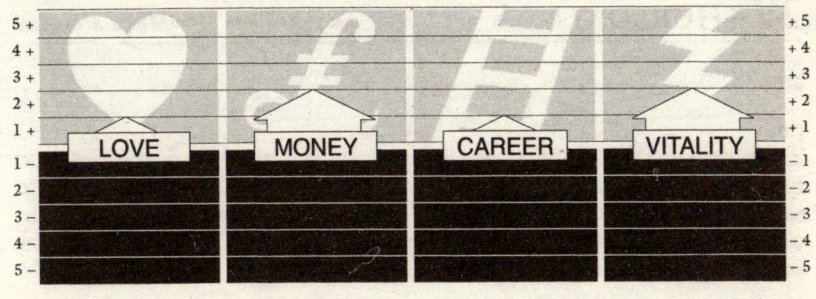

26 MONDAY

Moon Age Day 8   Moon Sign Cancer

am . . . .

pm . . . .
You start the week being able to display a great deal of vivacity and you
could be so very capable that others will almost instantly turn to you for
advice. This is Aquarius at its very best, so be prepared to turn heads
wherever you go. Be careful though, because you can still be just a little
too outspoken for your own good.

27 TUESDAY

Moon Age Day 9   Moon Sign Cancer

am . . . .

pm . . . .
You now have a chance to set your thoughts on widening your horizons
as much as you can. Some of this may have to do with work, but there
may also be a strong desire for travel. If going very far proves difficult for
now, you can plan ahead, and for the moment even short excursions
would do you a great deal of good.

28 WEDNESDAY

Moon Age Day 10   Moon Sign Leo

am . . . .

pm . . . .
Today could indicate a low point for Aquarius, though how difficult this
turns out to be is almost certainly down to the way you deal with it. The
lunar low this month does nothing to prevent you from thinking, though
it could impose certain physical limitations. Work with these instead of
against them and you can ensure all is well.

29 THURSDAY

Moon Age Day 11   Moon Sign Leo

am . . . .

pm . . . .
Even if financial and practical matters receive a good deal of input, you
may not be in the right frame of mind to deal with it. Don't be afraid to
shelve things you don't want to sort out today and enjoy some time spent
either alone or with one very special person. Trying to bulldoze
situations at the moment simply will not work.

30 FRIDAY
Moon Age Day 12   Moon Sign Leo

am . . . .

pm . . . .
This is the third day in a row during which you need to be more circumspect and steady than usual. Fortunately the lunar low will be out of the way for the weekend and in any case as today advances, the positive qualities of life begin to show again. Social trends for the evening look positive, so why not make the most of them?

31 SATURDAY
Moon Age Day 13   Moon Sign Virgo

am . . . .

pm . . . .
You have scope to be very expressive and outgoing today. All traces of the hesitation and doubt that were evident towards the end of the working week can be banished, and you should know exactly how to get what you want in most situations. Aquarius can be very attractive at the moment and can get into the limelight.

1 SUNDAY
Moon Age Day 14   Moon Sign Virgo

am . . . .

pm . . . .
Trends suggest a strong desire for personal freedom, and you can be quite fidgety if you don't have the chance to follow your own desires today. Travel and cultural matters are of great significance right now, and the strong intellectual qualities you possess make you shy away from anything that seems ignorant or lacking in finesse.

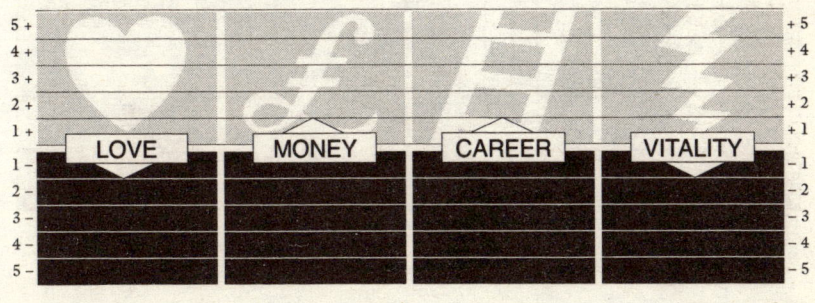

April 2007

YOUR MONTH AT A GLANCE

⊕ = Opportunities are around   ⊖ = Be on the defensive   ⬤ = Life is pretty ordinary

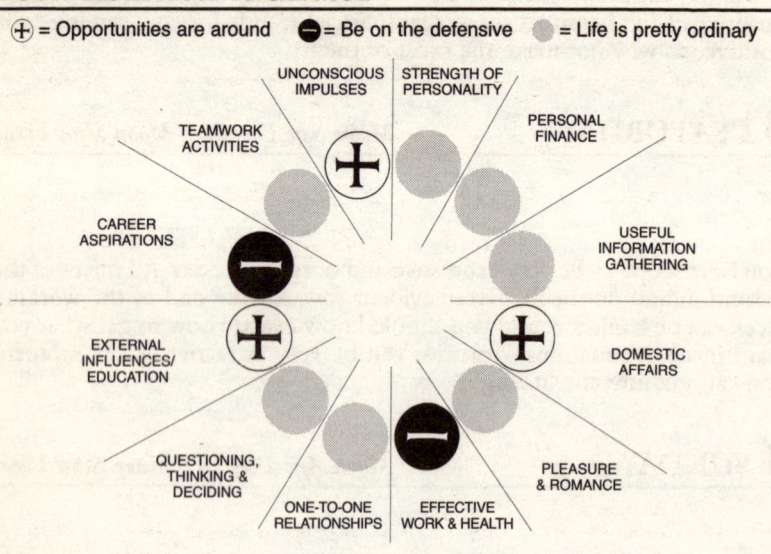

UNCONSCIOUS IMPULSES

STRENGTH OF PERSONALITY

TEAMWORK ACTIVITIES

PERSONAL FINANCE

CAREER ASPIRATIONS

USEFUL INFORMATION GATHERING

EXTERNAL INFLUENCES/ EDUCATION

DOMESTIC AFFAIRS

QUESTIONING, THINKING & DECIDING

PLEASURE & ROMANCE

ONE-TO-ONE RELATIONSHIPS

EFFECTIVE WORK & HEALTH

APRIL HIGHS AND LOWS

Here I show you how the rhythms of the Moon will affect you this month. Like the tide, your energies and abilities will rise and fall with its pattern. When it is above the centre line, go for it, when it is below, you should be resting.

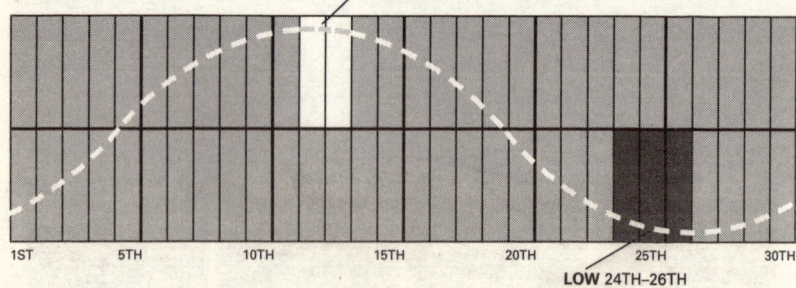

HIGH 12TH–13TH

1ST   5TH   10TH   15TH   20TH   25TH   30TH

LOW 24TH–26TH

2 MONDAY
Moon Age Day 15   Moon Sign Libra

am ....

pm ....
In terms of your career you could be entering a week of fits and starts. If you really want to get on, it will be important to deal with matters one at a time and to make sure each is sorted before you move on. Things should be less problematical in personal attachments, which can be made entirely secure by the actions you take now.

3 TUESDAY
Moon Age Day 16   Moon Sign Libra

am ....

pm ....
Today could be favourable for planning all sorts of entertainments and also for getting out into the world beyond your door. Aquarians generally like the spring and a lot of fresh air is definitely good for you, so it's worth making the most of any good weather that is about. Even a short walk at lunchtime would be better than nothing.

4 WEDNESDAY
Moon Age Day 17   Moon Sign Libra

am ....

pm ....
You can remain generally optimistic and able to get others to do your bidding without bullying them in any way. You often show a great interest for the old, curious or downright odd, and this could well be the case at the moment. Now is the time to keep a watchful eye on spending and curb the extravagant tendencies of others.

5 THURSDAY
Moon Age Day 18   Moon Sign Scorpio

am ....

pm ....
You should not have to try too hard in order to bring others round to your particular point of view at present. With a generally charming attitude and a classless approach to life, Aquarius can always be at the forefront of activities and can achieve popularity. Even if not everyone loves you today, those who don't can probably be ignored.

6 FRIDAY

Moon Age Day 19   Moon Sign Scorpio

am . . . .

pm . . . .
Mercury is now in your solar fourth house, encouraging you to limit what you are saying to those within your immediate circle. You could be slightly less inclined to be interfering with the world at large and can take greater delight in events that take place behind closed doors and within your own castle keep.

7 SATURDAY

Moon Age Day 20   Moon Sign Sagittarius

am . . . .

pm . . . .
The weekend should be steady, though you can step up the pace if you fancy a more eventful time. It is possible that you will be content to watch and wait, or to go shopping. Aquarius loves luxury and this certainly seems to be the case at the moment. In personal attachments you can show yourself to be very sensitive.

8 SUNDAY

Moon Age Day 21   Moon Sign Sagittarius

am . . . .

pm . . . .
This has potential to be a most attractive time when it comes to friends and lovers. You have scope to be as charming as ever, anxious to please and filled with delight by the smallest things. Creature comforts should appeal and you have what it takes to surround yourself with tasteful objects and people who stimulate your mind.

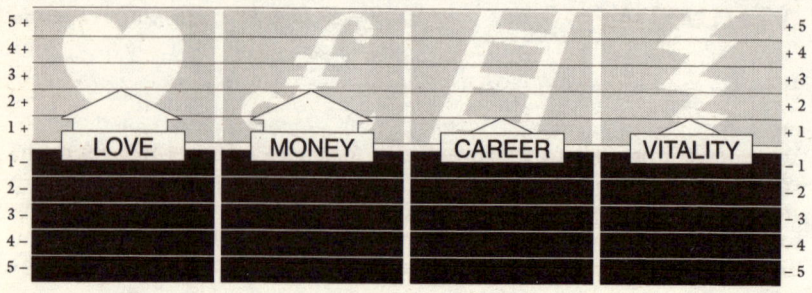

9 MONDAY · *Moon Age Day 22 · Moon Sign Sagittarius*

am . . . .

pm . . . .
This could well be the start of a very good period on the home front and a time when you can afford to turn your mind in the direction of ways to make yourself more comfortable. There are some slight financial gains possible, even if these come not as a result of your own efforts but as a result of luck.

10 TUESDAY · *Moon Age Day 23 · Moon Sign Capricorn*

am . . . .

pm . . . .
Getting your own way with others ought to be within your capabilities today, but you can also be quite sensitive at the moment so you are unlikely to use those around you for your own ends. You can find ways and means to feather your own nest, while also doing what you can to make the lives of others better too.

11 WEDNESDAY · *Moon Age Day 24 · Moon Sign Capricorn*

am . . . .

pm . . . .
With a slightly quieter interlude on offer today, you should have time to stop and think. There are gains to be made from adopting a contemplative frame of mind, and you can plan for a much racier period that will come across the next few days. You can persuade relatives to offer you some support.

12 THURSDAY · *Moon Age Day 25 · Moon Sign Aquarius*

am . . . .

pm . . . .
There ought to be much around that will motivate you now, and the lunar high brings new incentives, as well as allowing you to firm up decisions you have already made. If it seemed like a long way to the winning post only a couple of days ago, now you can make sure it is clearly within your sight.

13 FRIDAY
Moon Age Day 26   Moon Sign Aquarius

am ....

pm ....
Your opinions count at the moment – so much so that you might decide
to give advice to almost everyone! You have what it takes to seek a place
in the social limelight and to surround yourself with new possibilities in
a professional sense. Acting on impulse can sometimes be dangerous, but
it seems to be a way of life at the moment.

14 SATURDAY
Moon Age Day 27   Moon Sign Pisces

am ....

pm ....
Your ability to communicate your true feelings to loved ones is very well
marked today. If you know very well that a heart-to-heart is long
overdue, you could do worse than to instigate it sometime today. Trends
bestow on you a light touch when dealing with subordinates or younger
family members.

15 SUNDAY
Moon Age Day 28   Moon Sign Pisces

am ....

pm ....
This is a very favourable time for working in groups and also for getting
to grips with any issues that confused you last week. New hobbies are
possible, and you have scope to make your home surroundings more
comfortable in some way. Your practical judgements are likely to be
sound under present influences.

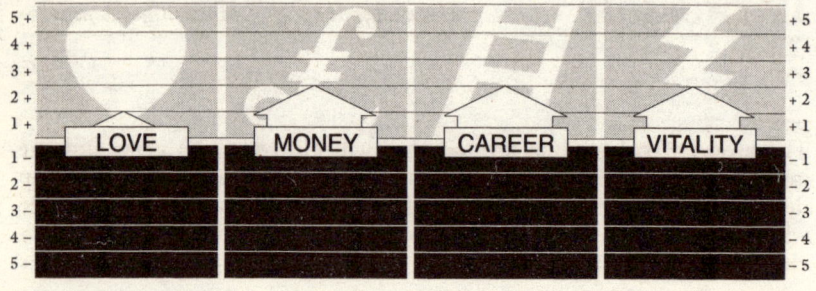

16 MONDAY   *Moon Age Day 29   Moon Sign Aries*

am . . . .

pm . . . .
Balancing your time commitments could prove to be rather difficult at
the start of this working week. It could seem as though everyone is
demanding your attention during every minute. This would be a
problem to some zodiac signs, but you have the mind of a juggler and
can cope, even when the pressure is really on.

17 TUESDAY   *Moon Age Day 0   Moon Sign Aries*

am . . . .

pm . . . .
The present position of the Sun in your solar chart shows this to be a very
good time for getting to grips with domestic issues and also for directing
the actions of younger family members. If you remain very approachable,
you should encourage people to seek you out for the sort of advice you
find easy to offer.

18 WEDNESDAY   *Moon Age Day 1   Moon Sign Taurus*

am . . . .

pm . . . .
You really do need to make room in your life for doing what you want,
rather than what seems expedient. There are some interesting encounters
possible, some of which may be totally unexpected. Beware of being too
quick to react to what sounds like an insult because you could have things
entirely wrong.

19 THURSDAY   *Moon Age Day 2   Moon Sign Taurus*

am . . . .

pm . . . .
Your strength today lies in the tremendous help you can give to a friend
or even a close relative. There are strong aspects in your solar chart that
emphasise your ability both to listen and to offer sound advice. Even if it
means putting yourself out a great deal, you can afford to help almost
anyone who seems to be in a pickle.

20 FRIDAY

Moon Age Day 3   Moon Sign Gemini

am . . . .

pm . . . .
Work and practical matters get a boost from the present position of both
Venus and Mars in your solar chart. Why not end the working week with
a flourish and show what you are made of socially by being willing to
stand out in any crowd? Look out for some small gains, even if these are
not necessarily of a financial nature.

21 SATURDAY

Moon Age Day 4   Moon Sign Gemini

am . . . .

pm . . . .
Even if you think quickly and react positively this weekend, there is a
dreamy side to your nature that seems to have little to do with your
normal state of mind at the moment. You could also be very nostalgic
and much more likely than has been the case recently to hold on to
precious memories.

22 SUNDAY

Moon Age Day 5   Moon Sign Cancer

am . . . .

pm . . . .
Be prepared to spend at least part of today doing what comes naturally
to you and don't worry too much about progressing. Some good social
and personal opportunities could be lost if you insist on pushing forward
all the time, and even Aquarius cannot keep going at break-neck speed
indefinitely.

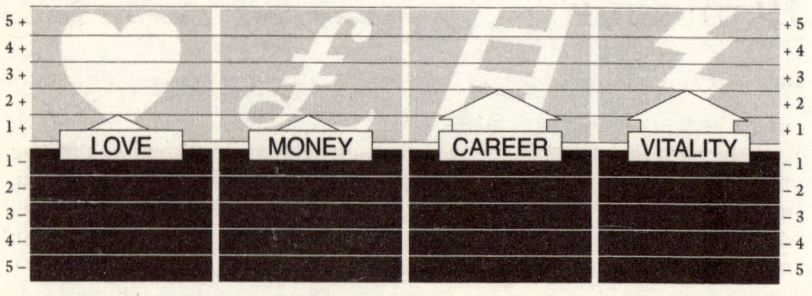

23 MONDAY   *Moon Age Day 6   Moon Sign Cancer*

am . . . .

pm . . . .
This is the last day before a short period during which you may feel much
more withdrawn and far less inclined to push yourself forward. By all
means get what you can done but delegate some jobs, because by
tomorrow you are entering a less progressive state. Routines that seem
tedious today will be comfortable later.

24 TUESDAY   *Moon Age Day 7   Moon Sign Leo*

am . . . .

pm . . . .
Getting plenty of rest is a good idea between now and the end of the
week. This is not to suggest that you are totally lacking in energy, merely
that you need to protect yourself a little more than would normally be
the case. The lunar low could help you to be more approachable, because
for once you are probably not rushing around everywhere.

25 WEDNESDAY   *Moon Age Day 8   Moon Sign Leo*

am . . . .

pm . . . .
There could be some hold-ups today and it would be advisable to deal
with situations one at a time, ensuring that you have achieved all you can
before moving on. If the attitude of colleagues and friends is difficult to
interpret, you might have to ask more questions than would usually be
the case.

26 THURSDAY   *Moon Age Day 9   Moon Sign Leo*

am . . . .

pm . . . .
For the third day in a row the Moon is in your opposite zodiac sign, but
not for too long. Even if things start out quietly, as the day progresses
you have what it takes to return to your old self. By the evening you
could be advertising your presence again and getting fully involved in
social ventures.

27 FRIDAY

Moon Age Day 10   Moon Sign Virgo

am . . . .

pm . . . .
There is a continued positive focus on your family life, together with a real insight into the motivations of others generally. You might even seem to be rather psychic at the moment, assisting you to predict how almost anyone will react. This can be a very fortunate gift when it comes to business matters.

28 SATURDAY

Moon Age Day 11   Moon Sign Virgo

am . . . .

pm . . . .
With so much planetary energy focused on the positive things of life, no wonder you can make a good impression this weekend. Although you show great flexibility, it would still be sensible to stick in the main to what you know and understand. Much time can be lost simply coming to terms with new situations.

29 SUNDAY

Moon Age Day 12   Moon Sign Libra

am . . . .

pm . . . .
Trends assist you to enjoy being number one in a social sense and to use this Sunday to further your intentions at home and also with regard to romance. It seems as though everything you do is custom-designed to get you noticed and you shine well in company. All of this helps you to achieve contentment.

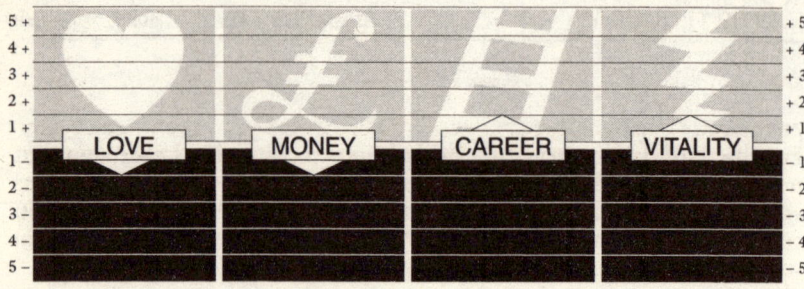

30 MONDAY

Moon Age Day 13   Moon Sign Libra

am . . . .

pm . . . .
This is a good time for professional developments, and Aquarians who
are between jobs at present need to keep their eyes wide open now. With
everything to play for financially you can pursue ways of increasing your
income, even if the outcome of your plans lays some way in the future.

1 TUESDAY

Moon Age Day 14   Moon Sign Libra

am . . . .

pm . . . .
Discussions and friendly encounters are well starred as May gets started.
Being part of a group seems to work well for you at present and you are
in a position to give a great deal of thought to improving your
surroundings, both at home and at work. Aquarians can now show their
easy-going and casual side.

2 WEDNESDAY

Moon Age Day 15   Moon Sign Scorpio

am . . . .

pm . . . .
A day to seek out pleasure and novelty wherever and whenever you can.
You can add to your stock of intelligence now by being willing to ask the
right questions and by focusing on matters that others find difficult to
address. Any sort of puzzle or mystery has potential to captivate you both
now and in the days ahead.

3 THURSDAY

Moon Age Day 16   Moon Sign Scorpio

am . . . .

pm . . . .
Your mind is sharp and your powers of perception have rarely been better
than they seem to be at the moment. A word of caution however: there
are still moments during which the wool can be pulled over your eyes,
particularly if you are not paying quite enough attention to what is going
on in a specific sense.

4 FRIDAY
Moon Age Day 17   Moon Sign Sagittarius

am . . . .

pm . . . .
You can afford to be dreamy and imaginative today, and may also be thinking about new ways in which to divert your mind. A certain restless steak is in evidence, though this can be dealt with by looking at matters that are new and interesting. What Aquarius seems to need most right now is travel.

5 SATURDAY
Moon Age Day 18   Moon Sign Sagittarius

am . . . .

pm . . . .
Dealing with others in a generally harmonious way, you now do everything in your power to increase your popularity. This is almost certainly not a conscious matter, but needing to be liked is part of your basic make-up. Family-minded Aquarians would be wise to spend time with relatives rather than friends today.

6 SUNDAY
Moon Age Day 19   Moon Sign Sagittarius

am . . . .

pm . . . .
You can make this another fairly harmonious and happy sort of day, though you may be more restless and have a strong need to ring the changes somehow. Rules and regulations could get on your nerves, and you will be at your best when you are free to decide what you want to do moment by moment.

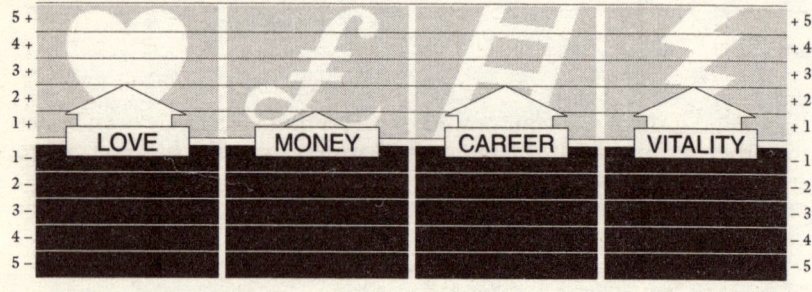

May 2007

YOUR MONTH AT A GLANCE

⊕ = Opportunities are around ⊖ = Be on the defensive ⬤ = Life is pretty ordinary

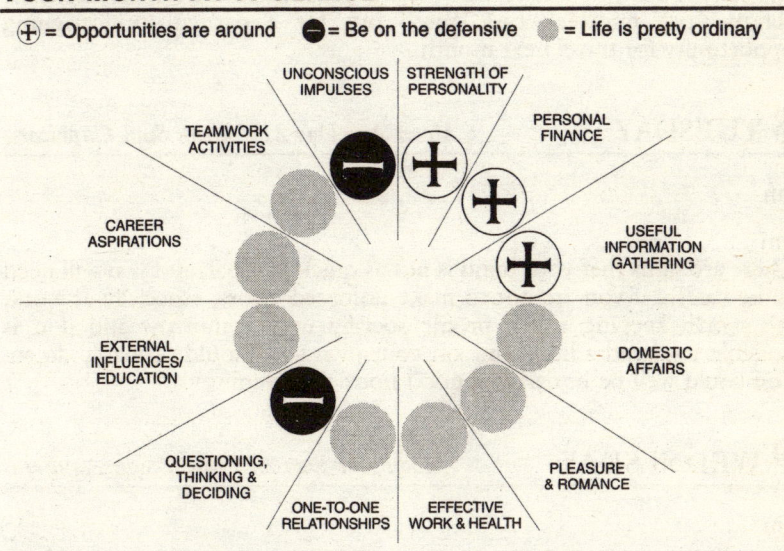

MAY HIGHS AND LOWS

Here I show you how the rhythms of the Moon will affect you this month. Like the tide, your energies and abilities will rise and fall with its pattern. When it is above the centre line, go for it, when it is below, you should be resting.

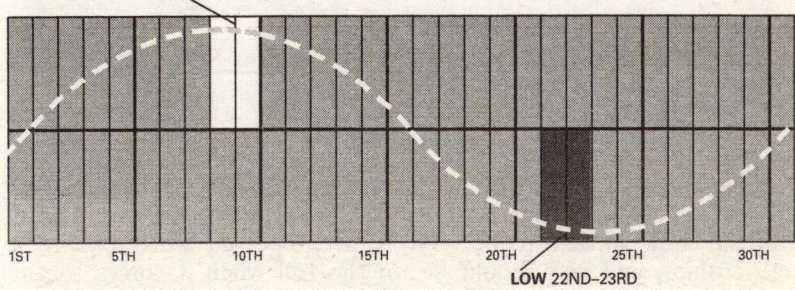

HIGH 9TH–10TH

LOW 22ND–23RD

7 MONDAY
Moon Age Day 20   Moon Sign Capricorn

am . . . .

pm . . . .
There are some interesting possibilities on offer early in the week, but
you may feel a little lethargic and not inclined to follow up on them. Why
not take some time out to think things through and clear the decks for
action from midweek on? Watch out for a particularly intriguing
opportunity for travel next month.

8 TUESDAY
Moon Age Day 21   Moon Sign Capricorn

am . . . .

pm . . . .
There are signs that your mind is not as quick as usual, and you will need
to be careful if you are not to make unforced errors, especially at work.
It's worth keeping a low profile socially until tomorrow and if it is
possible to spend a little time on your own you should probably do so.
You could well be buried in a good book this evening!

9 WEDNESDAY
Moon Age Day 22   Moon Sign Aquarius

am . . . .

pm . . . .
What you encounter today might be little more than good luck, but
make the best of positive trends whilst they are around and follow up on
new incentives. People can be persuaded to follow your lead, and you
needn't be afraid to dump outmoded concepts or issues that are no
longer relevant.

10 THURSDAY
Moon Age Day 23   Moon Sign Aquarius

am . . . .

pm . . . .
Positive spirits are a legacy of the continuing lunar high, and you may be
willing to take on any amount of work whilst you are feeling so energetic.
You can show yourself to be very creative, especially when looking at
relationships, and you should be on the ball when it comes to any
potential advancement at work.

11 FRIDAY

Moon Age Day 24   Moon Sign Pisces

am . . . .

pm . . . .
Beware of being too rash for your own good. The problem is that you might be tempted to speak out without thinking much in advance. This could land you in some hot water, and you will need to react quickly in order to get out of trouble. Fortunately you are well equipped for thinking on your feet.

12 SATURDAY

Moon Age Day 25   Moon Sign Pisces

am . . . .

pm . . . .
If there is something you want from a friend or a family member this may be the best day of the month to ask them. Not only do you have a good deal of cheek, you are also blessed with strong persuasive powers. Doing favours for others comes quite naturally, and you should also be very tidy-minded at present.

13 SUNDAY

Moon Age Day 26   Moon Sign Pisces

am . . . .

pm . . . .
Much of May shows you to be less family-oriented than might sometimes be the case, and you have scope to get a great deal from friends, one or two of whom are making a return visit to your life. Many of the values you hold in common with others display themselves in quite a marked manner at present.

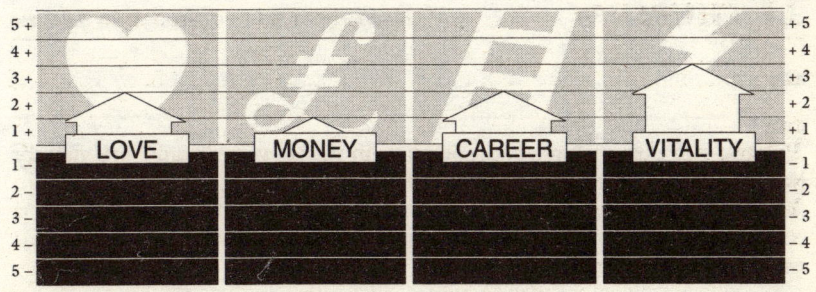

14 MONDAY

Moon Age Day 27   Moon Sign Aries

am . . . .

pm . . . .
You are entering a week that has a great deal of offer in a social sense, and even if you are applying yourself very well at work, it is those hours you spend away from responsibility that have potential to be the most rewarding. Energy levels remain especially high, offering you a chance to be quite sporting in attitude.

15 TUESDAY

Moon Age Day 28   Moon Sign Aries

am . . . .

pm . . . .
Trends indicate that you might have to deal with some restlessness that is rising within your nature at present. Staying put and concentrating on the same old things probably won't appeal to you at all. It could be the arrival of the early summer or simply the planetary trends, but whatever the cause you need to move about.

16 WEDNESDAY

Moon Age Day 29   Moon Sign Taurus

am . . . .

pm . . . .
As a direct contrast to yesterday the present position of the Moon encourages you to be lazy, though in a very specific way. Instead of interfering with everything, you may be much more inclined to watch and wait. You can make this trend pay off for you, particularly if it relieves you of some arduous tasks.

17 THURSDAY

Moon Age Day 0   Moon Sign Taurus

am . . . .

pm . . . .
A domestic relationship or some situation within your immediate vicinity has potential to become more of an issue today. You will require flexibility and understanding in order to deal well with others and need to exhibit more patience. Any nagging doubts you feel at the present time probably have no basis in fact.

18 FRIDAY   *Moon Age Day 1   Moon Sign Gemini*

am . . . .

pm . . . .
Venus is in a good position to stimulate your sense of style and also your
need for luxury. You may not take kindly to having to tackle dirty or
unsavoury jobs at present and might decide to delegate such things to
others whenever you can. Getting on side with a colleague who is
presently filled with good ideas would be no bad thing.

19 SATURDAY   *Moon Age Day 2   Moon Sign Gemini*

am . . . .

pm . . . .
When you are faced with something that genuinely interests you it should
be easy to race for the finishing line, but the same cannot be said of jobs
that you see as boring or without purpose. There is room for you to leave
such things to others, though you need to be careful that you are not
accused of laziness.

20 SUNDAY   *Moon Age Day 3   Moon Sign Cancer*

am . . . .

pm . . . .
A day to be bold, brave and determined when faced with any sort of
challenge. This shouldn't be difficult because you are clearly in the
market for stretching yourself – though once again, only when it suits
your purposes to do so. Trends suggest you won't take kindly to being
told what to do by anyone today.

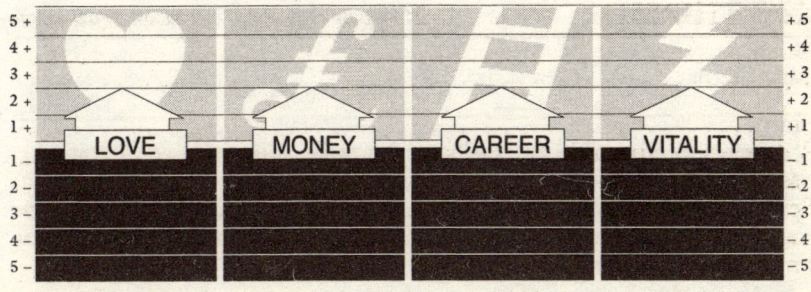

21 MONDAY
Moon Age Day 4   Moon Sign Cancer

am . . . .

pm . . . .
The start of this working week may be slightly quieter than usual. The Moon is working its way towards the zodiac sign of Leo and that means the arrival of the lunar low. Make the most of a less stressful interlude by tidying up aspects of the past, ahead of a new surge coming later in the month.

22 TUESDAY
Moon Age Day 5   Moon Sign Leo

am . . . .

pm . . . .
Even if positive and new possibilities are in evidence all around you, for the moment you may feel less than inclined to become involved. Your best approach is to treat today and tomorrow as being nothing more than an interlude during which you have time to contemplate life. Everyone needs a break now and again, and Aquarius is no exception.

23 WEDNESDAY
Moon Age Day 6   Moon Sign Leo

am . . . .

pm . . . .
This is a time during which you have an opportunity to wind down certain energetic activities. Turn the lunar low to your advantage. The year is advancing and the flowers are growing. You can afford to spend some time with your partner or a family member and walk in a meadow. Such little outings can help you to revitalise your soul.

24 THURSDAY
Moon Age Day 7   Moon Sign Virgo

am . . . .

pm . . . .
Success should come more easily to you today and you have what it takes to get right back on form, especially when in company. You relish the presence of interesting and informative people in your life and should be working hard to achieve specific objectives. Most important of all you might find it easier to concentrate now.

25 FRIDAY
Moon Age Day 8   Moon Sign Virgo

am . . . .

pm . . . .
It might seem as though certain circumstances are working against your best interests now, but this isn't necessarily the case. All the more reason to look at things from a different angle and try to be both original and inventive. It shouldn't be long before you discover that you can turn misfortune to your advantage.

26 SATURDAY
Moon Age Day 9   Moon Sign Virgo

am . . . .

pm . . . .
Be prepared to work hard and decide in advance what your objectives for the day should be. Originality is the key to success and you are not short of that commodity. Personal relationships can prove to be very interesting at the moment and you might even discover an admirer you didn't know you had.

27 SUNDAY
Moon Age Day 10   Moon Sign Libra

am . . . .

pm . . . .
Beware of overestimating your capabilities today. If you know you are somehow out of your depth, this would be a good time to seek some expert advice. You may well be in the mood for shopping and there might be things you will want to get done at home. This has potential to be a busy but generally rewarding day.

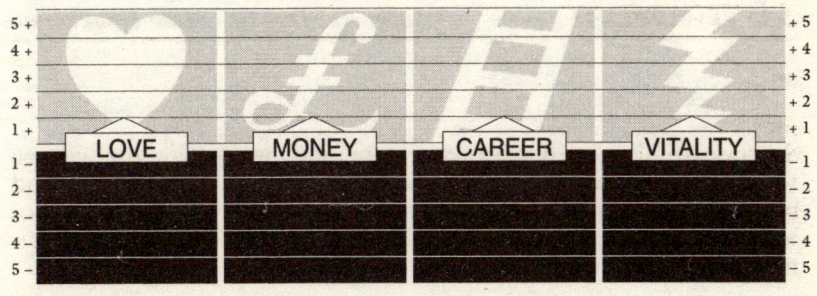

28 MONDAY · *Moon Age Day 11 · Moon Sign Libra*

am . . . .

pm . . . .
Compromise is very important at the start of this week. The position of
the planet Mars in your solar chart suggests obstinacy, and you may be
less inclined to seek a path that is both reasonable and realistic. Despite
any difficulties, you would be wise to avoid going out on a limb or
committing yourself to too many jobs.

29 TUESDAY · *Moon Age Day 12 · Moon Sign Scorpio*

am . . . .

pm . . . .
Practical issues should be easier to deal with now and you can show a
great deal of tolerance when dealing with others. If colleagues are quite
demanding, you have the ability to look to their humanity and to show
great sensitivity to the needs of others generally. Routines can be a drag
but they may be necessary.

30 WEDNESDAY · *Moon Age Day 13 · Moon Sign Scorpio*

am . . . .

pm . . . .
This is an excellent time to get yourself out into the social mainstream,
impressing people and making new friends. Don't get overconfident at
work and be willing to settle for second-best in at least one case. All in
all, you are probably better off tackling situations one at a time and head-
on whenever possible at present.

31 THURSDAY · *Moon Age Day 14 · Moon Sign Scorpio*

am . . . .

pm . . . .
New ideas and altered perspectives are nothing new to the average
Aquarian. Today you excel when it comes to looking at alternatives, and
you carry the opinions of others with you because of your powers of
persuasion. An ideal time to get in touch with people who may be far
away from you at present.

1 FRIDAY

Moon Age Day 15   Moon Sign Sagittarius

am . . . .

pm . . . .
You continue to show a very kind and considerate face to the world at large and this attitude holds you in good stead. What may well be the end of the working week for you is best spent consolidating recent gains, rather than trying too hard to push situations even further. You would be wise to seek a steady sort of day.

2 SATURDAY

Moon Age Day 16   Moon Sign Sagittarius

am . . . .

pm . . . .
Though optimism might seem to be in abundance, it's possible that you are somewhat hesitant right now. You may decide that you need constant reassurance from others, and will be checking the attitude of family members and friends on a very regular basis. It's worth getting organised with family obligations.

3 SUNDAY

Moon Age Day 17   Moon Sign Capricorn

am . . . .

pm . . . .
You can afford to settle for a steady sort of Sunday, and needn't be too quick to get involved in issues that could lead to arguments later. You need to be kindness itself and if you are you could discover that those around you will do anything to please you. The Moon is now in your solar twelfth house, so rushing around may not seem appealing.

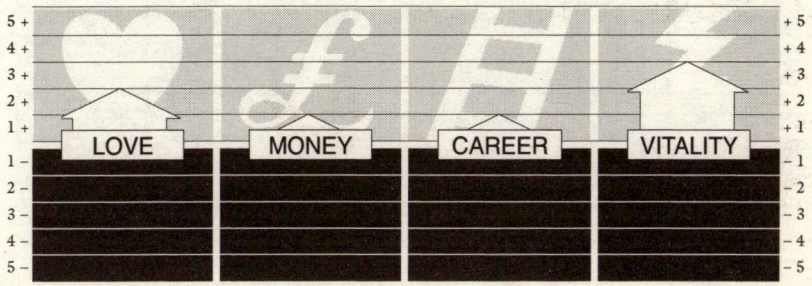

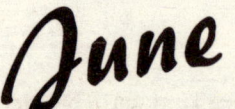 2007

YOUR MONTH AT A GLANCE

⊕ = Opportunities are around ⊖ = Be on the defensive ⬤ = Life is pretty ordinary

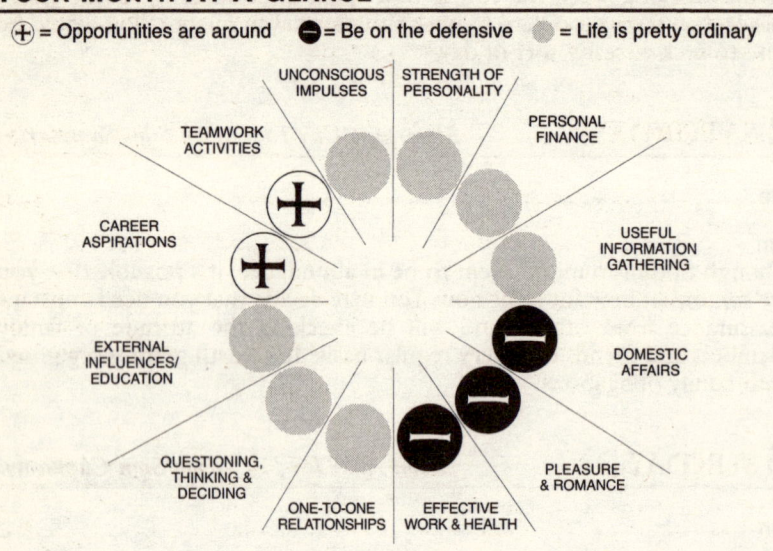

JUNE HIGHS AND LOWS

Here I show you how the rhythms of the Moon will affect you this month. Like the tide, your energies and abilities will rise and fall with its pattern. When it is above the centre line, go for it, when it is below, you should be resting.

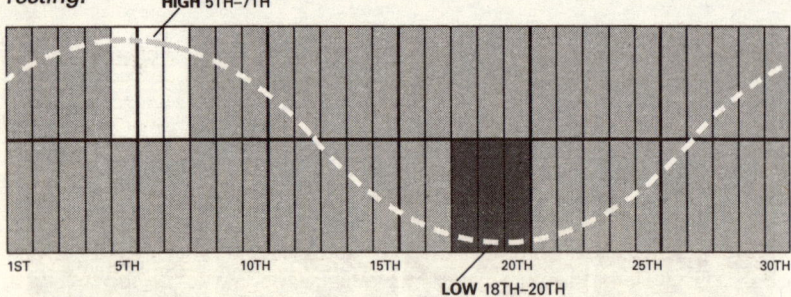

90

4 MONDAY *Moon Age Day 18   Moon Sign Capricorn*

am . . . .

pm . . . .
Instead of firing from the hip when it comes to discussions or even arguments, why not listen carefully to what others are saying? Compromise is possible, and you will do yourself a favour if you accept this fact. Aquarius can be very awkward to deal with at the moment, but thankfully this is nothing but a short interlude.

5 TUESDAY *Moon Age Day 19   Moon Sign Aquarius*

am . . . .

pm . . . .
The lunar high will come along at just the right time for most of you. You need a physical and mental boost and that is what you can take advantage of today. Revitalised, and with masses of energy at your disposal, you should be in a position to look towards brightening your future and feathering your nest financially.

6 WEDNESDAY *Moon Age Day 20   Moon Sign Aquarius*

am . . . .

pm . . . .
Optimism should be in abundance now, and as long as it is not misplaced, you can do a great deal with it. Today responds best if you concentrate on things you know instinctively to be important and leave other matters until later. You have a tremendous ability to get things done today, but this gift should not be squandered.

7 THURSDAY *Moon Age Day 21   Moon Sign Aquarius*

am . . . .

pm . . . .
You should still be on a roll, and can use today's opportunities to make the lot of your friends easier. When it comes to romance you should also be on top form. The compliments flow from you like honey, and if you are at the very beginning of a relationship the situation should look especially good.

8 FRIDAY

Moon Age Day 22   Moon Sign Pisces

am . . . .

pm . . . .
Optimism remains your middle name, even though the lunar high is now finished. Steady and realistic, but still able to move at least small mountains, the pace you are setting yourself is sensible and welcomed by others. A day to avoid getting bogged down with any sort of red tape, especially at work.

9 SATURDAY

Moon Age Day 23   Moon Sign Pisces

am . . . .

pm . . . .
Today offers you scope to look towards those things that are both realistic and practical, and in this way you can make headway with your life generally. Aquarius is not always this sensible, but it pays dividends when you are. You may well have family members and friends clamouring for your attention at the moment.

10 SUNDAY

Moon Age Day 24   Moon Sign Aries

am . . . .

pm . . . .
Intimate relationships count for a great deal now, and you may decide it would be very pleasant to spend some time alone with your partner or sweetheart. Even if you remain generally active, it's worth slowing down enough to watch the flowers grow on what can be a very happy sort of June Sunday.

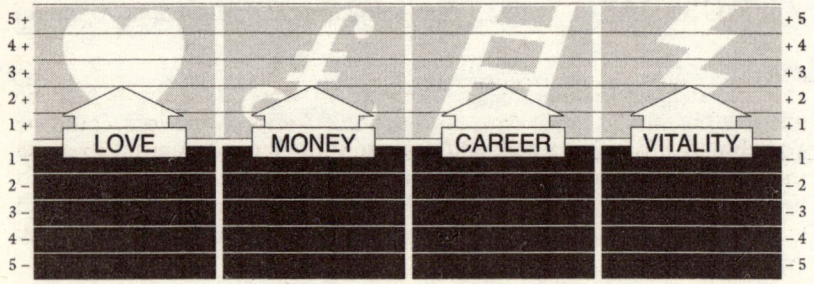

11 MONDAY *Moon Age Day 25   Moon Sign Aries*

am . . . .

pm . . . .
Joint finances can be strengthened now, and you have it within you to
organise yourself very well at the moment. You can keep life fairly steady,
and your natural tendency to react positively to situations seems to be in
place. Attitude is very important when dealing with professional matters.

12 TUESDAY *Moon Age Day 26   Moon Sign Taurus*

am . . . .

pm . . . .
There may be something slightly wrong at home, though this is unlikely
to be as a result of your attitude or actions. Maybe you just can't see eye-
to-eye with other family members, or have different ideas about the way
forward with regard to domestic changes. Whatever the reason, your best
response is to talk about it.

13 WEDNESDAY *Moon Age Day 27   Moon Sign Taurus*

am . . . .

pm . . . .
Even if on a personal level you feel lively, you also have it within you to
be quiet and contemplative. This is a day that needs to be divided into
compartments and a time when you can more easily come to terms with
the attitudes and opinions of those with whom you live.

14 THURSDAY *Moon Age Day 28   Moon Sign Gemini*

am . . . .

pm . . . .
Considerable improvements are possible at work, even if these have
nothing specifically to do with your actions. A little more luck could be
available, and you can afford to speculate more than has been the case
recently. Romance is well highlighted later in the day.

15 FRIDAY

Moon Age Day 0   Moon Sign Gemini

am . . . .

pm . . . .
Today is good for communications and for getting to know people who might be of use to you a little further down the line. Be certain before you commit yourself to a major change, and in fact it might be sensible to put such matters on hold for a day or two. Socially speaking you have potential to be on top form.

16 SATURDAY

Moon Age Day 1   Moon Sign Cancer

am . . . .

pm . . . .
In terms of personal attachments it is time to show how loyal and supportive you are capable of being. In a more practical sense you need to consider cutting your losses over an issue that you can't alter any more and moving on to things over which you do have an influence. Why not opt for a journey today if it proves to be possible?

17 SUNDAY

Moon Age Day 2   Moon Sign Cancer

am . . . .

pm . . . .
Now you can capitalise on favourable trends associated with travel of any sort and can also be very sharp when in company. Your active mind goes this way and that, assisting you to respond very well to intellectual discussions and to anything associated with current affairs and your locality.

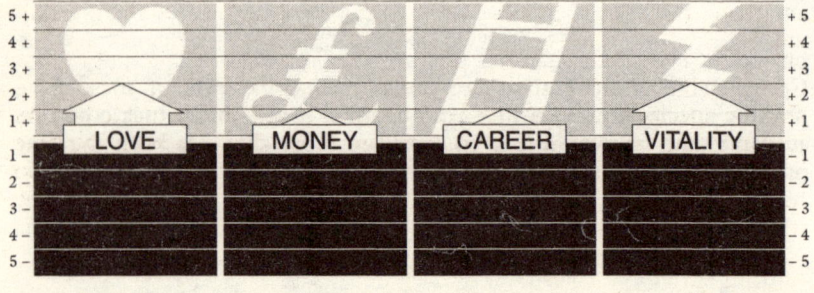

18 MONDAY · *Moon Age Day 3 · Moon Sign Leo*

am . . . .

pm . . . .
You may decide to rethink a certain project at the start of this working week, and should have sufficient time to do so now that the lunar low has arrived. Don't make any irrevocable decisions for the moment, but watch and wait. You can obtain help if you need it, but you could be rather too proud to ask.

19 TUESDAY · *Moon Age Day 4 · Moon Sign Leo*

am . . . .

pm . . . .
Taking actions without sufficient consideration could lead you to slight problems for the moment. Once again you need to be very careful and to address new situations as cautiously as you can. The start of new projects might be best put on hold until you are sure that they are what you need in order to progress.

20 WEDNESDAY · *Moon Age Day 5 · Moon Sign Leo*

am . . . .

pm . . . .
For the first part of today at least the influence of the lunar low is present. This suggests proceeding with caution and allowing others to take some of the strain. By tomorrow you can get right back on form, so spending today clearing the decks for more positive actions would be no bad thing.

21 THURSDAY · *Moon Age Day 6 · Moon Sign Virgo*

am . . . .

pm . . . .
Certain information you can glean from associates could prove to be very interesting today, and you can use it to get back up to speed in no time at all. Even the most casual remark can set you thinking and you seem to have what it takes to bring others round to your specific point of view without really trying.

22 FRIDAY
Moon Age Day 7   Moon Sign Virgo

am . . . .

pm . . . .
You are now able to look forward to benefits that come from partnerships of various sorts. This could be associated with business but it just as likely to relate to personal attachments. It would appear that this is a fine time for mixing business with pleasure, and maybe even for starting a business project of your own.

23 SATURDAY
Moon Age Day 8   Moon Sign Libra

am . . . .

pm . . . .
Even if you are on a definite winning streak, you may have to back off in terms of career now that the weekend has arrived. Slowing your mind down won't be easy, which is why you need to get it busy dealing with matters that are of personal rather than practical interest. You can persuade friends to be warm and receptive today.

24 SUNDAY
Moon Age Day 9   Moon Sign Libra

am . . . .

pm . . . .
Family responsibilities are highlighted under present astrological trends, but you needn't let these weigh heavily on your mind. You can take great delight in the successes that others are achieving, and you will do all you can to support family members – particularly younger people.

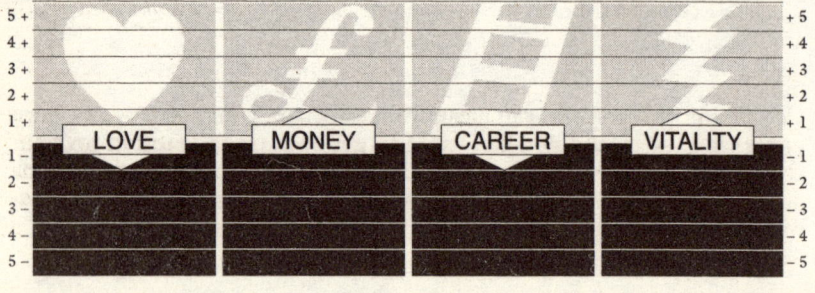

25 MONDAY   *Moon Age Day 10   Moon Sign Libra*

am . . . .

pm . . . .
Positive influences surround you on all sides, making the start of a new
working week an ideal period in which to push yourself a little more. You
don't know what you are capable of achieving until you try, and there
should be ample opportunity to flex your business muscles over the next
few days.

26 TUESDAY   *Moon Age Day 11   Moon Sign Scorpio*

am . . . .

pm . . . .
You have what it takes to be an exciting person to be around. The planet
Mars is now in a particularly good position to offer more bite to your
nature, though from its position in your solar sixth house it needn't make
you too caustic or in any way unapproachable. Routines will probably
hold little interest for you now.

27 WEDNESDAY   *Moon Age Day 12   Moon Sign Scorpio*

am . . . .

pm . . . .
It seems that you can get a great deal from a range of different people at
present, and you needn't look at anything too deeply. The reason for this
lies in the fact that there is so much around that takes your interest. You
can afford to be a 'grazer' at the moment, especially with new facts that
surround your life.

28 THURSDAY   *Moon Age Day 13   Moon Sign Sagittarius*

am . . . .

pm . . . .
There is good potential for relationships of a personal nature today and
you can use all aspects of romance to make you feel more comfortable
and secure. You may not be quite as impressive in a social sense as seems
to have been the case during the last few days, but you could be especially
warm with one specific person.

29 FRIDAY

Moon Age Day 14   Moon Sign Sagittarius

am . . . .

pm . . . .
Emotional attachments could now prove to be warmer and more secure than ever and you may not really want to move far from home today. If you decide to make a move you should be able to settle to whatever you have to do very well, but might not show quite the flexibility of nature that often typifies the average Aquarian.

30 SATURDAY

Moon Age Day 15   Moon Sign Capricorn

am . . . .

pm . . . .
A quieter interlude is possible for the weekend, but this is not something that is imposed upon you. If you are more reflective and less socially active this is because you want to be this way and not because of any undue pressures that are being brought to bear on you. You can find time for a real family discussion this weekend.

1 SUNDAY

☿   *Moon Age Day 16   Moon Sign Capricorn*

am . . . .

pm . . . .
You have scope to show just how caring you are today, and to make sure that your considered opinions are valuable to others. Look for new skills now, especially in terms of hobbies and pastimes. Someone you don't see very often may be making an appearance on the periphery of your life, and their presence should be welcome.

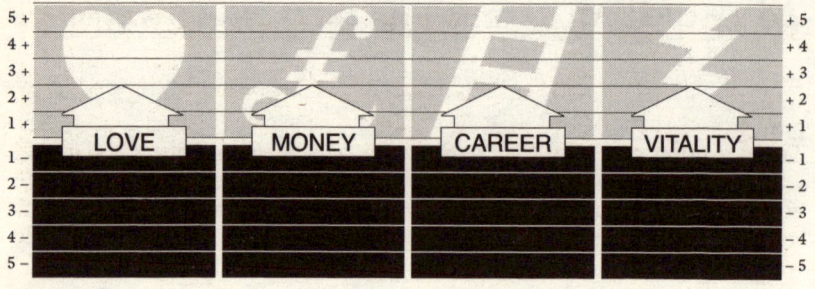

July 2007

YOUR MONTH AT A GLANCE

⊕ = Opportunities are around   ⊖ = Be on the defensive   ⬤ = Life is pretty ordinary

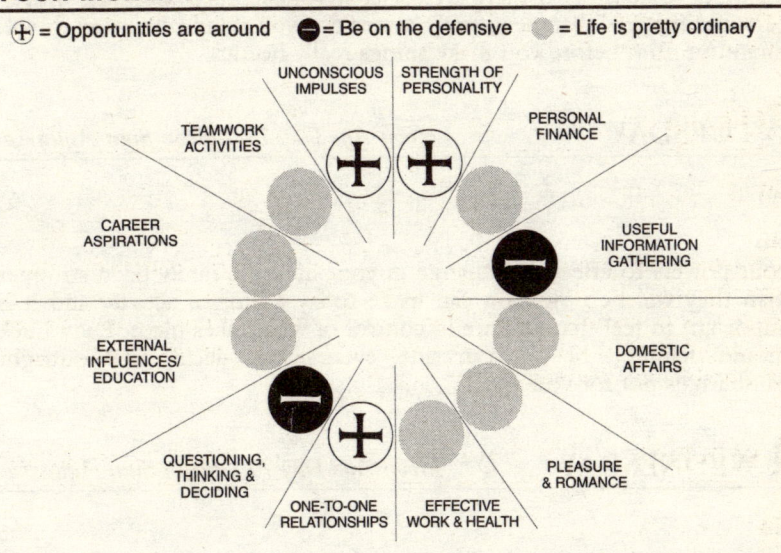

UNCONSCIOUS IMPULSES

STRENGTH OF PERSONALITY

TEAMWORK ACTIVITIES

PERSONAL FINANCE

CAREER ASPIRATIONS

USEFUL INFORMATION GATHERING

EXTERNAL INFLUENCES/ EDUCATION

DOMESTIC AFFAIRS

QUESTIONING, THINKING & DECIDING

ONE-TO-ONE RELATIONSHIPS

EFFECTIVE WORK & HEALTH

PLEASURE & ROMANCE

JULY HIGHS AND LOWS

Here I show you how the rhythms of the Moon will affect you this month. Like the tide, your energies and abilities will rise and fall with its pattern. When it is above the centre line, go for it, when it is below, you should be resting.

HIGH 3RD–4TH   HIGH 30TH–31ST

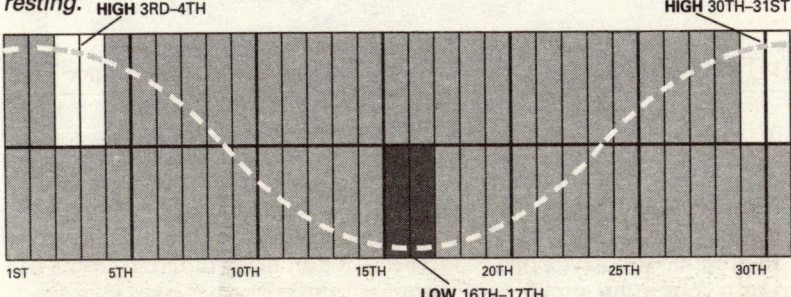

1ST   5TH   10TH   15TH   20TH   25TH   30TH

LOW 16TH–17TH

2 MONDAY ☿ *Moon Age Day 17* *Moon Sign Capricorn*

am . . . .

pm . . . .
Get yourself ready because busier times are possible soon. You might have some moments for reflection today, but these are likely to be the last for quite some time. If there are social arrangements to be dealt with or personal matters that need your attention, you would be wise to sort them out now, before you make things really hectic!

3 TUESDAY ☿ *Moon Age Day 18* *Moon Sign Aquarius*

am . . . .

pm . . . .
Your powers to effect real change in your life have rarely been stronger than they will be now. You can make today a blur of activity and it is important to feel that you are in control of what takes place. Lady Luck should definitely be on your side, even if you decide that outright gambling is not for you.

4 WEDNESDAY ☿ *Moon Age Day 19* *Moon Sign Aquarius*

am . . . .

pm . . . .
The positive trends continue and now you can make the most of any situation that puts you in the social mainstream. You have what it takes to mix well with all manner of people and may even manage to forge an alliance with someone you haven't cared for in the past. Personalities could well enter your life around now.

5 THURSDAY ☿ *Moon Age Day 20* *Moon Sign Pisces*

am . . . .

pm . . . .
Plenty of comings and goings are possible today, because although the lunar high is now finished the positive planetary trends supporting it are still present. You have potential to be active on many different fronts and to turn your fertile mind in just about any direction that takes your fancy.

6 FRIDAY ☿ *Moon Age Day 21   Moon Sign Pisces*

am . . . .

pm . . . .
At this time you need not be short of interesting company, and the end of the working week for many of you brings with it some fascinating possibilities for later. Once work is out of the way you can set out to enjoy yourself. You can make the evening extremely entertaining, particularly if you are at your amusing best.

7 SATURDAY ☿ *Moon Age Day 22   Moon Sign Aries*

am . . . .

pm . . . .
It might seem in some ways that home is the best place to be for the first part of this weekend, though you probably won't take much persuading that this is not the case. If you have an opportunity to be gadding about again, you may take special pleasure from shopping or visiting a place of historic or scenic interest.

8 SUNDAY ☿ *Moon Age Day 23   Moon Sign Aries*

am . . . .

pm . . . .
Trends suggest that certain aspects of your life deserve more thought than you have afforded them of late. Even if you are still very keen to be out there in the social mainstream, there is also something that tends to call you back. The only sensible way forward is to split your time so that both facets of your mind get an equal airing.

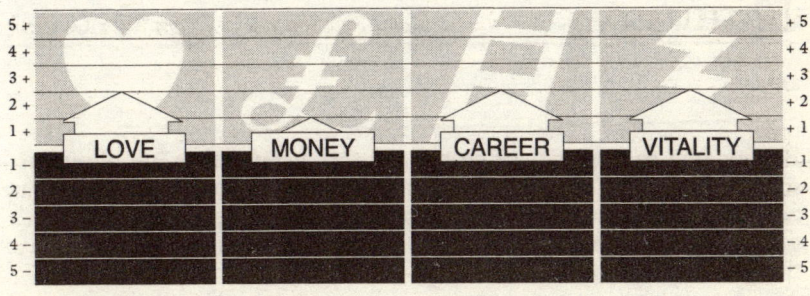

9 MONDAY
☿ *Moon Age Day 24 Moon Sign Taurus*

am . . . .

pm . . . .
The emphasis at the moment seems to be on one-to-one relationships, offering an opportunity for you to spend some time looking at how you can improve them. Family concerns may also be uppermost in your mind and although you have what it takes to work hard, your mind may often be elsewhere.

10 TUESDAY
☿ *Moon Age Day 25 Moon Sign Taurus*

am . . . .

pm . . . .
You can afford to remain happily on the go for most of today and need not be quite so concerned about specific issues as seems to have been the case yesterday. If people are generally kind in their approach, the likelihood of the situation is that you are only getting from them what you give in the first place.

11 WEDNESDAY
Moon Age Day 26 Moon Sign Gemini

am . . . .

pm . . . .
Even if you have got most aspects of life fairly settled, your emotional responses might be somewhat odd. You don't get the messages from your partner that you might expect and could in any case be rather more sensitive than is good for you. Your best approach is to avoid taking things too seriously or too literally.

12 THURSDAY
Moon Age Day 27 Moon Sign Gemini

am . . . .

pm . . . .
Be prepared to display your charm and seek happiness in just about any sort of company. One of the greatest gifts of the Aquarian nature is your adaptability, and it certainly seems to be in evidence at present. It's worth giving yourself some time out for simple enjoyment and to enjoy what the season has to offer.

13 FRIDAY
Moon Age Day 28   Moon Sign Cancer

am . . . .

pm . . . .
In general daily life might seem to take on a fairly routine quality and if you want any excitement you will probably have to arrange it for yourself. Now is the time to do something different and unexpected, if only to keep others guessing for a while. The evening has good social potential, but once again it's up to you.

14 SATURDAY
Moon Age Day 29   Moon Sign Cancer

am . . . .

pm . . . .
Why not put some zip into your Saturday and do what you can to cheer up family members and friends? You should be very good at bringing people out of their shells and can also persuade those around you that they are more confident and capable then they think. In matters of love you have what it takes to show great sensitivity and kindness.

15 SUNDAY
Moon Age Day 0   Moon Sign Cancer

am . . . .

pm . . . .
If you are on holiday at the moment you have clearly chosen a good time to take a break. Even if this is not the case you can look for opportunities to do something different and interesting on this high summer Sunday. Rather than settling for pointless routines, don't be afraid to ring the changes whenever you get the chance.

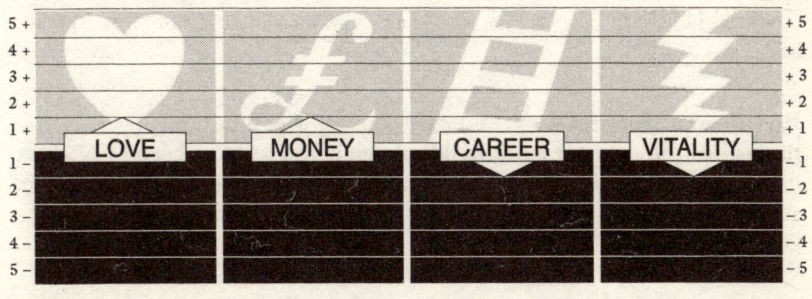

16 MONDAY
Moon Age Day 1   Moon Sign Leo

am . . . .

pm . . . .
The start of a new working week coincides with the lunar low and you may not be able to make too much practical headway for the moment. It would be better to settle for what you know and understand, rather than trying to push yourself into areas that are going to create unnecessary problems.

17 TUESDAY
Moon Age Day 2   Moon Sign Leo

am . . . .

pm . . . .
Today responds best if you rely on those around you, rather than trying to accomplish everything for yourself. The advantage of this time is that what you believe about yourself falls far short of reality, so even the lunar low can be turned to your advantage when you do make some progress.

18 WEDNESDAY
Moon Age Day 3   Moon Sign Virgo

am . . . .

pm . . . .
Trends encourage you to take the lead in romantic matters, and although the middle of a working week might seem to be a fairly unlikely time to sweep someone off their feet, you do have that ability. You probably won't have much time for petty rules or officious people under present planetary influences.

19 THURSDAY
Moon Age Day 4   Moon Sign Virgo

am . . . .

pm . . . .
Partnerships and affairs of the heart take priority now, and this may also have a bearing on your working life. Even if you want to keep busy at the moment, you might not have quite everything you need to take decisions you know to be of great importance. If in doubt, you can afford to ask a colleague or a friend for help.

20 FRIDAY *Moon Age Day 5   Moon Sign Libra*

am . . . .

pm . . . .
There are some important peaks to be reached before the working week
comes to a close. You can show yourself to be very capable and well able
to make the right decisions. If you are between jobs at the moment you
could do much worse that to conduct a search today, because this
interlude offers definite possibilities.

21 SATURDAY *Moon Age Day 6   Moon Sign Libra*

am . . . .

pm . . . .
All varieties of partnership take on a new significance this weekend. These
may be personal attachments, sporting associations or even business ties,
but whatever they are, the planets are shining for them. Getting along
well with almost anyone is your forte, and you can show the fact now.

22 SUNDAY *Moon Age Day 7   Moon Sign Libra*

am . . . .

pm . . . .
You have scope to make meetings with others rather pleasurable, and to
turn your mind towards ways and means of having fun. You are
humorous, inclined to play practical jokes on others and should be very
good company to have around. A favourable time to bring newcomers
into your social fold.

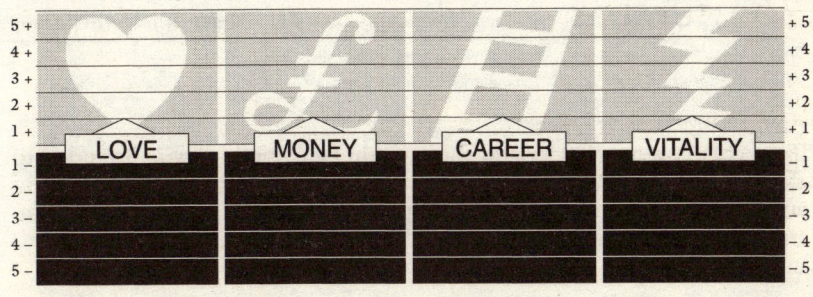

23 MONDAY
Moon Age Day 8   Moon Sign Scorpio

am . . . .

pm . . . .
The feelings of a loved one can have a great bearing on your thought patterns at the start of this working week. Time and again your mind is inclined to return to family concerns, even when there is little or nothing to be concerned about. People from the past may also be figuring strongly in your thinking.

24 TUESDAY
Moon Age Day 9   Moon Sign Scorpio

am . . . .

pm . . . .
In affairs of the heart you can make use of periods of sudden magnetic attraction, though these could just turn out to be slightly embarrassing if you find yourself receiving offers you didn't expect. You would be wise to make your true feelings clear from the start in any contact with others or you may also inspire unnecessary jealousy.

25 WEDNESDAY
Moon Age Day 10   Moon Sign Sagittarius

am . . . .

pm . . . .
Trends encourage you to be fairly happy with your lot and quite willing to take the rough with the smooth when at work. If you are pulling your weight, you can also get colleagues to do all they can to help you out, and for some Aquarians at the moment your general popularity seems to be going off the scale.

26 THURSDAY
Moon Age Day 11   Moon Sign Sagittarius

am . . . .

pm . . . .
The week is getting older and there might be something you intended to do that has been shelved or forgotten. Your best approach is to get on with it now and don't hedge or fudge when it would simply be easier to be direct and immediate. Once jobs you haven't been looking forward to are out of the way, you should feel almost liberated.

27 FRIDAY
Moon Age Day 12   Moon Sign Sagittarius

am . . . .

pm . . . .
Be prepared to get an early start today with all-important projects, and if you are going to be away from work during the weekend, do what you can today to set the seal on specific actions. It's really not worth leaving anything to chance and this also includes important details relating to future travel.

28 SATURDAY
Moon Age Day 13   Moon Sign Capricorn

am . . . .

pm . . . .
Standard responses to others probably won't work today and you might have your work cut out wondering why relatives and friends are behaving so oddly. Perhaps you should ignore their behaviour and simply get on with your own life. Anything with a distinctly intellectual bent could attract you at the moment.

29 SUNDAY
Moon Age Day 14   Moon Sign Capricorn

am . . . .

pm . . . .
This would be another very good day on which to follow your own incentives and ideas. Others can be persuaed to follow your lead, and although there are moments when you tend to be very reflective, you have what it takes to make most of the social arrangements and to make sure everyone is comfortable.

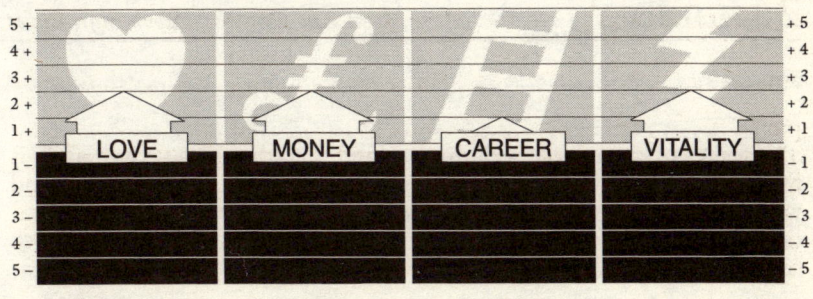

30 MONDAY
Moon Age Day 15   Moon Sign Aquarius

am . . . .

pm . . . .
Anything to do with travel can certainly help you to make life more interesting, and the lunar high also offers incentives you were not expecting. Turning even difficult situations to your advantage should be quite easy and you can be filled with enthusiasm for projects that seem custom-made to keep you happy.

31 TUESDAY
Moon Age Day 16   Moon Sign Aquarius

am . . . .

pm . . . .
A day to grasp every new opportunity with both hands, and don't squander the positive trends that stand around you now. Whether at work or at play you can be delightful to have around and can make new friends very easily at this time. When it comes to getting on with strangers you are in a really good position today.

1 WEDNESDAY
Moon Age Day 17   Moon Sign Pisces

am . . . .

pm . . . .
It looks as though you are now entering a much brisker period generally, but with the Moon in your solar fourth house you have scope to be committed to home and family too. The middle of this working week brings new incentives – though in reality some of them may have been around a while and you simply did not notice the fact.

2 THURSDAY
Moon Age Day 18   Moon Sign Pisces

am . . . .

pm . . . .
The forces of change are well in place and you can make sure that life is far from predictable or boring. This suits you down to the ground and you can move forward on all fronts with great enthusiasm and a good deal of energy. Not everyone can keep up with your lightning-quick thought processes, so be prepared to explain yourself.

3 FRIDAY
Moon Age Day 19   Moon Sign Aries

am . . . .

pm . . . .
When it comes to social interaction of any sort you have potential to be the undisputed master at the present time. Even if there is a lot to be done in a work sense it seems self-evident that you would rather play. Why not seek out like-minded people for new projects and soak up the compliments that you can attract?

4 SATURDAY
Moon Age Day 20   Moon Sign Aries

am . . . .

pm . . . .
One of your real talents at the moment is getting to the bottom of tricky situations and working out puzzles that others find impossible to master. You can make those in your vicinity marvel at your strong intuition and your ability to cut through red tape. This could well be a day of surprises and a time to think on your feet.

5 SUNDAY
Moon Age Day 21   Moon Sign Taurus

am . . . .

pm . . . .
The forces of change and transformation seem to be at work in your life, and if you readily commit yourself to alterations this is unlikely to be a problem. Those with whom you live could have more difficulty, and your interests are best served if you smooth the path for them as much as proves to be possible.

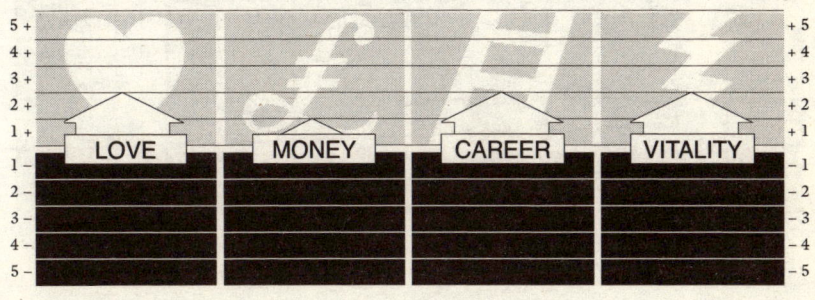

August 2007

YOUR MONTH AT A GLANCE

⊕ = Opportunities are around   ⊖ = Be on the defensive   ⬤ = Life is pretty ordinary

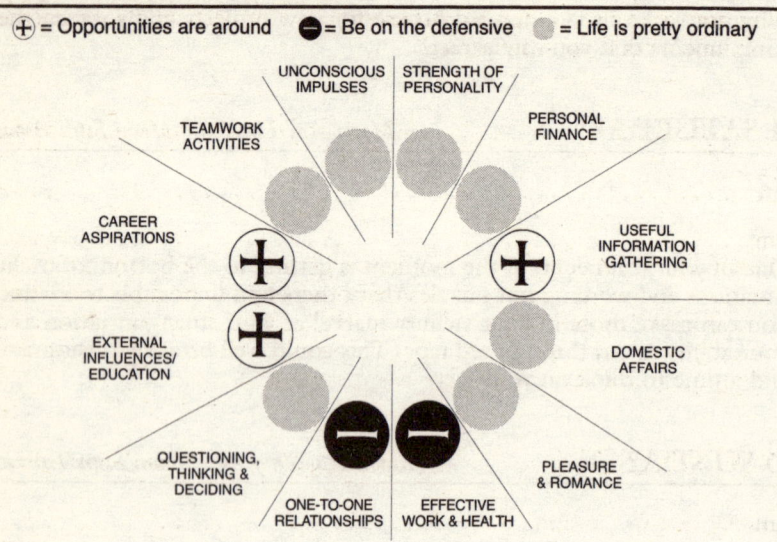

AUGUST HIGHS AND LOWS

§Here I show you how the rhythms of the Moon will affect you this month. Like the tide, your energies and abilities will rise and fall with its pattern. When it is above the centre line, go for it, when it is below, you should be resting.

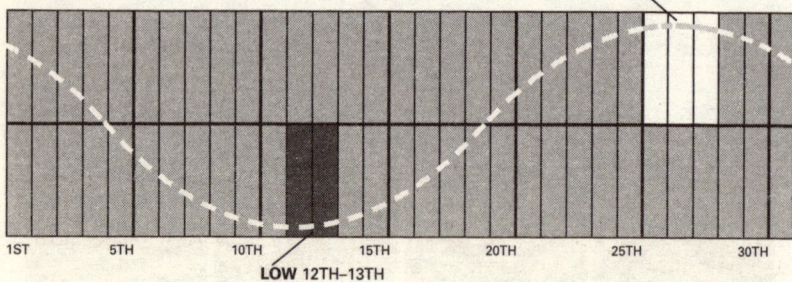

HIGH 26TH–28TH

LOW 12TH–13TH

1ST   5TH   10TH   15TH   20TH   25TH   30TH

6 MONDAY   *Moon Age Day 22   Moon Sign Taurus*

am . . . .

pm . . . .
All kinds of communications bring their own form of reward today. Be willing to talk to others and to make yourself available, even to those who have not always been particularly friendly in the past. You may decide to allow someone else to take on extra responsibility, particularly if it means a job won't get done otherwise.

7 TUESDAY   *Moon Age Day 23   Moon Sign Taurus*

am . . . .

pm . . . .
Pleasurable experiences are a possibility, most likely coming from the direction of your partner or close family members. The aspects relating to travel look good again, so maybe this is the time you should be thinking about taking a vacation. A day to enjoy the summer weather and if it rains, enjoy it anyway!

8 WEDNESDAY   *Moon Age Day 24   Moon Sign Gemini*

am . . . .

pm . . . .
You can achieve a good balance at the moment between the messages you are deliberately sending out, and the response you are getting in return. Not everyone may be working on your behalf today, but where it matters the most you have the ability to distinguish between the various motives in operation and react accordingly.

9 THURSDAY   *Moon Age Day 25   Moon Sign Gemini*

am . . . .

pm . . . .
It is very important at present to make a decision, even if you find out later that you were wrong in your basic estimations. Problems are more likely if you jump about from foot to foot. This may not be the best time for signing documents or dealing with legal matters.

10 FRIDAY
Moon Age Day 26   Moon Sign Cancer

am . . . .

pm . . . .
There are signs that the demands made on you professionally are likely to be significant now. That could be one of the reasons why you choose to commit yourself mainly to family matters. Certain issues could look somewhat threatening, and though you are not one to shy away from a challenge, you can't be on top form all the time.

11 SATURDAY
Moon Age Day 27   Moon Sign Cancer

am . . . .

pm . . . .
Even if practical matters go somewhat off course today, you should not allow this to prevent you from pushing forward with a will. Many of your ideas will fall by the wayside but it's the remaining ones that matter. Today responds best if you move ahead one step at a time and if you know you have a winner, put in that extra effort.

12 SUNDAY
Moon Age Day 28   Moon Sign Leo

am . . . .

pm . . . .
You could well have your work cut out with minor duties and tasks today and so might not want to cloud your horizons by looking too far ahead. That's fine. You need to be sure that you are all the details of life sorted and that you leave yourself with some time to think. Even the lunar low has its advantages.

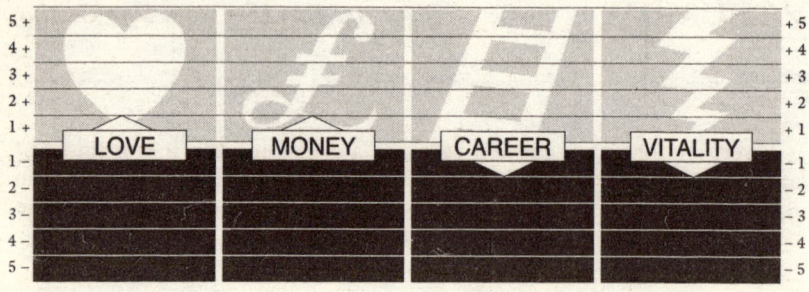

13 MONDAY
Moon Age Day 0   Moon Sign Leo

am . . . .

pm . . . .
Things may still not be going your way all the time, but you do have
scope to attract positive attention from the direction of friends and family
members. It's worth letting those around you make some of the running
this early in the week. In a day or two you can get yourself fully back on
form and be raring to go.

14 TUESDAY
Moon Age Day 1   Moon Sign Virgo

am . . . .

pm . . . .
It would be much better for all concerned if you let everyone know
exactly how you feel today. Of course your best approach is to do so in a
diplomatic manner, except in those cases when specific individuals really
don't want to listen. With them you might have to be blunt and really
speak your mind.

15 WEDNESDAY
Moon Age Day 2   Moon Sign Virgo

am . . . .

pm . . . .
You should now be in a position to get the most from romantic and
leisure possibilities. More settled inside yourself than seems to have been
the case for a few days, you may be quite willing to watch others struggle,
whilst you take a more contemplative and even matter-of-fact approach
to life generally.

16 THURSDAY
Moon Age Day 3   Moon Sign Virgo

am . . . .

pm . . . .
Communication with your partner, or someone else with whom you have
a particular affinity, allows you to get the heart of matters. In some ways
this appears to make the present period a slightly more serious one.
Nevertheless you can still find time for flippancy and fun, even if you have
to work harder than usual to smile.

17 FRIDAY

Moon Age Day 4   Moon Sign Libra

am . . . .

pm . . . .
You need to keep up the good work professionally. Once the needs of career are out of the way, you can set your sights on having fun. You can encourage people around you to join in and you certainly needn't go short of friends at present. You can afford to push your luck a little more under present planetary trends.

18 SATURDAY

Moon Age Day 5   Moon Sign Libra

am . . . .

pm . . . .
It is towards personal concerns that your mind is encouraged to turn now. Even if most aspects of your life are running smoothly, you can find something to worry about if you try hard enough. If you are conscious that this is what you are doing, it would be best to find ways and means of diverting your mind.

19 SUNDAY

Moon Age Day 6   Moon Sign Scorpio

am . . . .

pm . . . .
Long-standing commitments could well take up some of your time now. This might get in the way of what is essentially a socially motivated sort of Sunday. The way forward is to mix and match between what is necessary and the things you really want to do. Balance may not be easy to achieve now, but it is essential.

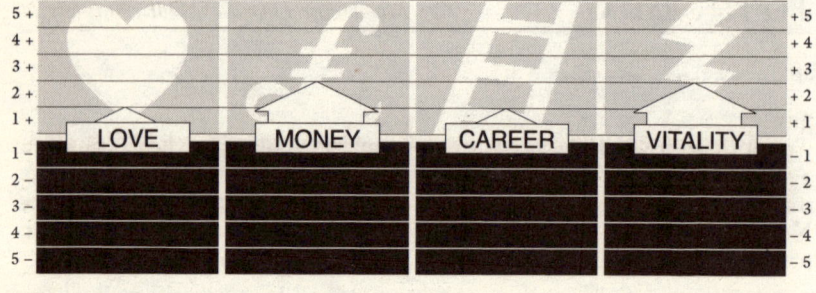

20 MONDAY
Moon Age Day 7   Moon Sign Scorpio

am . . . .

pm . . . .
Financial potential should be better than average today. Keep your wits about you and you have scope to make the most of small opportunities that come your way. Some advantage at work is also quite possible later in the day, and by the evening you can turn your mind to matters of a more personal nature.

21 TUESDAY
Moon Age Day 8   Moon Sign Scorpio

am . . . .

pm . . . .
A more extroverted period is now likely to be developing. You can use it to get your message across, and although there may still be some restrictions, there is the feeling that you are gaining the upper hand in particular situations. On those occasions when you feel out of your depth, it's worth asking for assistance.

22 WEDNESDAY
Moon Age Day 9   Moon Sign Sagittarius

am . . . .

pm . . . .
Today offers an opportunity to address any personal relationships that have recently been in the doldrums. Although you might still be finding it difficult to achieve the forward motion in your life that you would wish, there are definite signs that you can start to get things going your way. Friends could be especially supportive.

23 THURSDAY
Moon Age Day 10   Moon Sign Sagittarius

am . . . .

pm . . . .
Close encounters with people you haven't seen for quite some time could quite easily be the order of the day. For some this is deliberately engineered because it's possible that a distinctly nostalgic streak is running through you now. You have what it takes to offer timely assistance, especially within your family.

24 FRIDAY
Moon Age Day 11   Moon Sign Capricorn

am . . . .

pm . . . .
Group-related issues are once more to the fore. These don't come hard to you with your easy-going Air-sign ways. There are gains to be made if you get any important work out of the way as early in the day as you can. Later you can afford to turn your mind in the direction of the weekend and all that you have planned socially.

25 SATURDAY
Moon Age Day 12   Moon Sign Capricorn

am . . . .

pm . . . .
You will want to be as busy as possible today. In the midst of what has been a very stop-start sort of month it is important to react to the more positive moments. Refuse to be sidelined in discussions and insist on having your say. People should respect you all the more for doing so. Tomorrow offers much better overall prospects.

26 SUNDAY
Moon Age Day 13   Moon Sign Aquarius

am . . . .

pm . . . .
Stand by for the best of all worlds today. The Moon is in your zodiac sign and you should be feeling good. All in all you can make today your own. The time is right to go for what you want in life and not to accept any excuses, particularly from yourself. There is a real boost to your energy and a greater than usual sense of urgency.

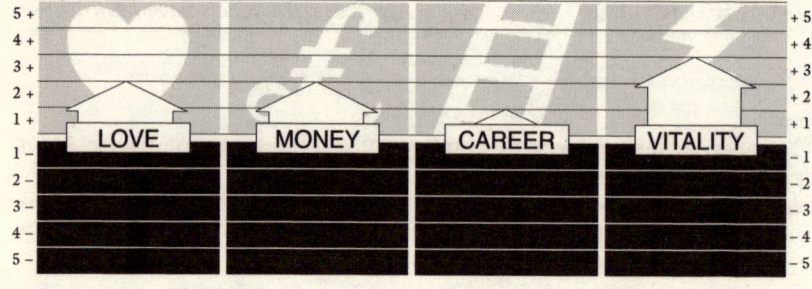

27 MONDAY   *Moon Age Day 14   Moon Sign Aquarius*

am . . . .

pm . . . .
The lunar high is all the more welcome after a month that may not have given you what you wanted for much of the time. Turning your mind today away from social matters and towards practical ones, you can show just how capable you are and will probably be happy to take decisions from which you might have shied away recently.

28 TUESDAY   *Moon Age Day 15   Moon Sign Aquarius*

am . . . .

pm . . . .
You can make this the third red-letter day in a row in terms of personal achievements. Of course you probably won't be able to do everything you would wish, but that shouldn't prevent you from having a try. Spending some time with friends and family members offers you scope to relish their company.

29 WEDNESDAY   *Moon Age Day 16   Moon Sign Pisces*

am . . . .

pm . . . .
For career-minded Aquarians this is one of the best periods imaginable, and the spirit of enterprise within you is well marked. Don't leave until tomorrow any job you can get out of the way today. Timely advice shouldn't be ignored, and you might even decide to hand out a few pearls of wisdom yourself.

30 THURSDAY   *Moon Age Day 17   Moon Sign Pisces*

am . . . .

pm . . . .
There is an opportunity to put yourself in the limelight today. Along comes a real boost to your spirits, even if you are mainly responsible for it yourself. Rather than getting tied down with responsibilities that are not rightfully yours, you would be wise to put most of your effort into new starts and thrilling possibilities.

31 FRIDAY
Moon Age Day 18   Moon Sign Aries

am . . . .

pm . . . .
There are nostalgic moments possible today, which is fine as long as you don't get obsessed with the past. Most of the really important aspects of your life still lie ahead of you. Some of them are around right now and you need to react positively to ensure that circumstances are turning in your direction.

1 SATURDAY
Moon Age Day 19   Moon Sign Aries

am . . . .

pm . . . .
You have a chance to let the home bird in you put in an appearance this weekend. This is one of the best periods of the year weather-wise and you can find plenty to do around the house and garden. If you decide that you must get out and about, spending time with friends whose presence makes you feel happier is an ideal choice.

2 SUNDAY
Moon Age Day 20   Moon Sign Taurus

am . . . .

pm . . . .
It looks as though you will get on better today when you are mixing and mingling. If you have to work across the weekend you should discover ways in which to combine business with pleasure, but if the day is your own you can show yourself to be on top form socially. A day to prove what a truly romantic individual you are.

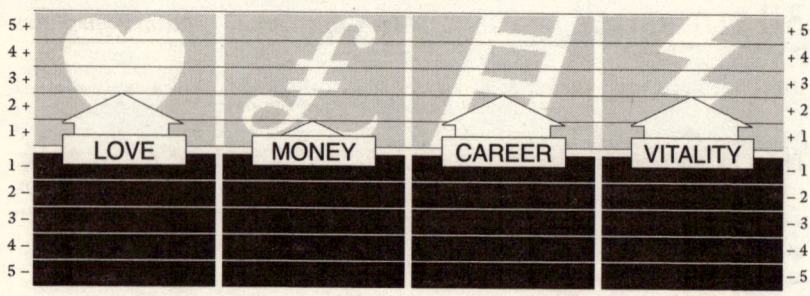

September

2007

YOUR MONTH AT A GLANCE

⊕ = Opportunities are around   ⊖ = Be on the defensive   ⬤ = Life is pretty ordinary

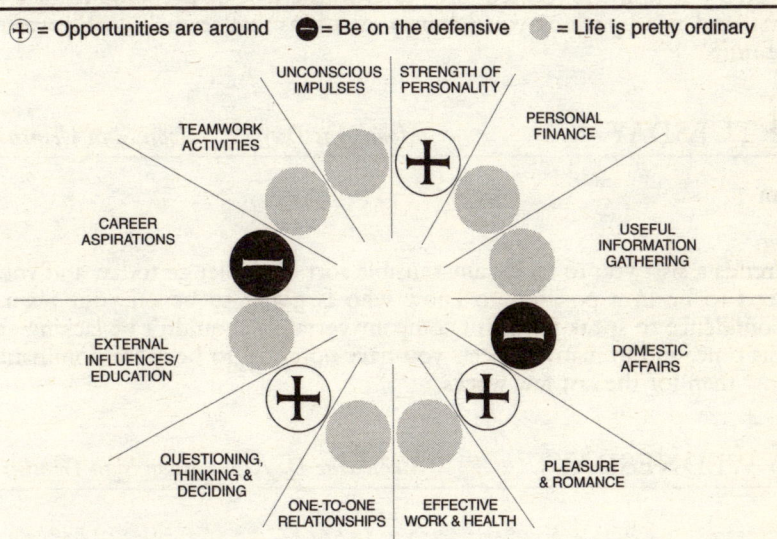

UNCONSCIOUS IMPULSES
STRENGTH OF PERSONALITY
PERSONAL FINANCE
TEAMWORK ACTIVITIES
CAREER ASPIRATIONS
USEFUL INFORMATION GATHERING
EXTERNAL INFLUENCES/ EDUCATION
DOMESTIC AFFAIRS
QUESTIONING, THINKING & DECIDING
PLEASURE & ROMANCE
ONE-TO-ONE RELATIONSHIPS
EFFECTIVE WORK & HEALTH

SEPTEMBER HIGHS AND LOWS

Here I show you how the rhythms of the Moon will affect you this month. Like the tide, your energies and abilities will rise and fall with its pattern. When it is above the centre line, go for it, when it is below, you should be resting.

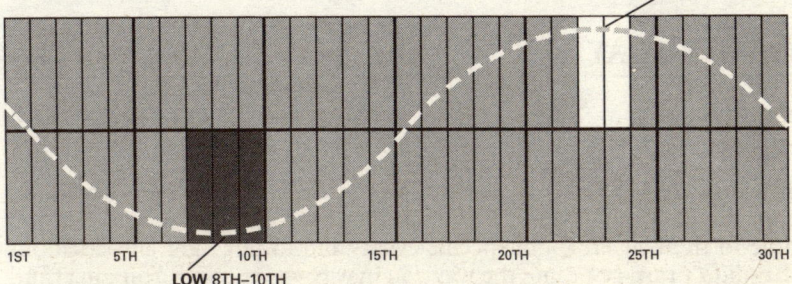

HIGH 23RD–24TH

1ST   5TH   10TH   15TH   20TH   25TH   30TH

LOW 8TH–10TH

3 MONDAY
Moon Age Day 21   Moon Sign Taurus

am . . . .

pm . . . .
You have what it takes to get the best from both career and personal matters now. Don't worry too much about details, most of which can be sorted out easily. If you feel tired later in the day, be prepared to take a rest, and avoid pushing yourself into situations that seem a terrible waste of time.

4 TUESDAY
Moon Age Day 22   Moon Sign Gemini

am . . . .

pm . . . .
Trends assisst you to tackle any sensible sort of challenge today, and you need to be in a position to know who is going to be on your team. Confidence to speak boldly in company certainly shouldn't be lacking at this time, and in many respects you have potential to be more dominant now than for the last few weeks.

5 WEDNESDAY
Moon Age Day 23   Moon Sign Gemini

am . . . .

pm . . . .
It's time for some light relief, even though you may be almost entirely committed to your working life today. The practical joker within you can be put on display, and you can get most people to go along with your off-the-wall sense of humour. Aquarius is out for fun, and you can extend this fact to your family life too.

6 THURSDAY
Moon Age Day 24   Moon Sign Cancer

am . . . .

pm . . . .
You may choose today to assess the progress you have been making in your life generally. Even if this is another busy sort of day, you can find time to think again about specific events and to put right any situations that didn't turn out quite the way you may have expected. You can afford to be very optimistic just now.

7 FRIDAY
Moon Age Day 25   Moon Sign Cancer

am . . . .

pm . . . .
Professional developments may now be going just a little off-course, especially if you are over-committed in some way. Try to plan ahead, particularly if you are thinking of making any changes at home. A journey might suit you this weekend, and if you haven't already arranged it, why not do so this evening?

8 SATURDAY
Moon Age Day 26   Moon Sign Leo

am . . . .

pm . . . .
Despite the lunar low you can immerse yourself fully in the social mainstream and do what you can to brighten the weekend, both for yourself and for the people you care about the most. You need to put in that extra little effort to get yourself ahead of the field, and could also be quite sporting at the moment.

9 SUNDAY
Moon Age Day 27   Moon Sign Leo

am . . . .

pm . . . .
Investing a great deal of confidence in others might occasionally lead to disappointments today. However, that's the way you are, and getting your fingers burnt now and again should not change your basic nature – thank goodness! If problems do come along, your best response is to deal with them cheerfully.

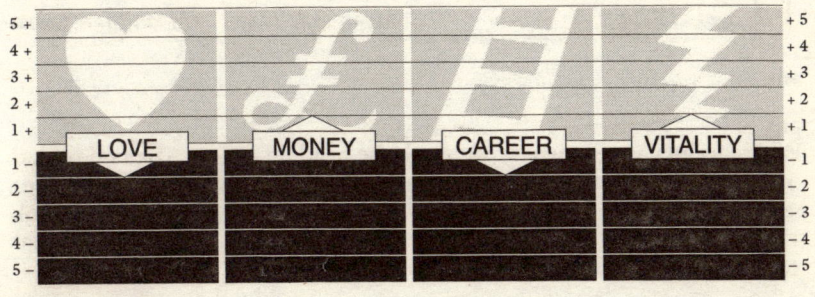

10 MONDAY
Moon Age Day 28   Moon Sign Leo

am . . . .

pm . . . .
The lunar low is still with you at the start of this new working week and you might decide to leave a few issues to others if your resources are more limited than usual. Attitude is very important when dealing with personal attachments, and you might not be too keen to commit yourself about anything long-term.

11 TUESDAY
Moon Age Day 29   Moon Sign Virgo

am . . . .

pm . . . .
It's possible that there is a tendency for you to look on the down side of situations for the moment. This is a situation that comes about as a result of the departing lunar low and is a trend that you can dispel during the day. If you keep yourself active socially you may get yourself out of the doldrums that much quicker.

12 WEDNESDAY
Moon Age Day 0   Moon Sign Virgo

am . . . .

pm . . . .
Teamwork situations can bring out the best in you and any temporary difficulties of the last few days should now be forgotten. The middle of the week can enable you to get closer to your heart's desire in one way or another and may also assist you to overcome a difficulty that has been around for a number of weeks.

13 THURSDAY
Moon Age Day 1   Moon Sign Libra

am . . . .

pm . . . .
Where money is concerned you could be heading for an extended period of potential increase. Although you might have to draw in your horns somewhat right now, this fact stands as evidence that you are able to look at financial matters more closely. By the weekend you can make sure that your position is generally more secure.

14 FRIDAY
Moon Age Day 2   Moon Sign Libra

am . . . .

pm . . . .
The emphasis today is on physical pleasures, and a general upturn in attitude is possible now. If you can persuade people to gather round to lend a helping hand, you should not be surprised if many jobs get done in a fraction of the time you might normally expect. Plan now for an exciting sort of weekend.

15 SATURDAY
Moon Age Day 3   Moon Sign Scorpio

am . . . .

pm . . . .
Getting out and about would work wonders as far as your general attitude is concerned today. Certainly you would be wise to avoid being cooped up in the same place for hours on end. Fresh fields and pastures new beckon. Aquarius is definitely in the mood for fun and can persuade everyone else to join in.

16 SUNDAY
Moon Age Day 4   Moon Sign Scorpio

am . . . .

pm . . . .
You may not deal too well with criticism today and tend to be rather more sensitive than usual. This can be the case even if you are not being attacked at all, and before you fly off the handle you need to look at situations very carefully. A day to keep abreast of local affairs and get involved in community projects.

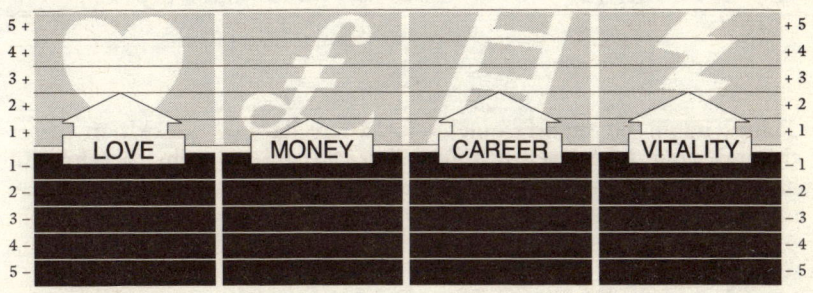

17 MONDAY   *Moon Age Day 5   Moon Sign Scorpio*

am . . . .

pm . . . .
Trends encourage a strong desire to get your ideas across to others today, and a few frustrations could follow if you find that you have some difficulty doing so. If people trivialise situations that are very important to you, your best approach is simply to exercise self-discipline.

18 TUESDAY   *Moon Age Day 6   Moon Sign Sagittarius*

am . . . .

pm . . . .
The planetary focus for today is on work and practical matters. You should be happy to talk to almost anyone and can be certain of eliciting the most positive of responses. Don't forget sporting activities and general ways of keeping physically fit. These are important under present trends.

19 WEDNESDAY   *Moon Age Day 7   Moon Sign Sagittarius*

am . . . .

pm . . . .
Even casual talks with others could prove enlightening during the present period. This might be especially true at work, with the possibility of promotion coming along for some Aquarians at this time. By all means keep your most entertaining side hidden until the evening, but do involve yourself then because there are happy times on offer.

20 THURSDAY   *Moon Age Day 8   Moon Sign Capricorn*

am . . . .

pm . . . .
Things might be slightly quieter for a few days, as the Moon passes through your solar twelfth house. You can still be quite cheerful and happy, but elements of the past could come into your mind and you may be more reflective than usual. Some time spent alone could be useful.

21 FRIDAY　　　　*Moon Age Day 9　Moon Sign Capricorn*

am . . . .

pm . . . .
You have scope to remain quieter but also optimistic and ready for almost anything life throws in your path. Workaday concerns are limited by your present state of mind and you should be quite happy to go with the flow in a social sense. Your emotional responses are generally positive, particularly if love is important to you at the moment.

22 SATURDAY　　　　*Moon Age Day 10　Moon Sign Capricorn*

am . . . .

pm . . . .
Before today is out the Moon will have moved into your own zodiac sign of Aquarius, though this does not take place until the late afternoon. This can mean a split sort of day, with quieter and more reflective responses predominating early on. By the time the sun sets, it is quite possible that you will be in the market for fun.

23 SUNDAY　　　　*Moon Age Day 11　Moon Sign Aquarius*

am . . . .

pm . . . .
If you work at the weekend you can make this one of the best days of the month. Most of your energies can now be given to practical matters, and thoughts about how you can get ahead are very predominant right now. Instead of avoiding controversy you can afford to embrace it, and do so with impunity most of the time.

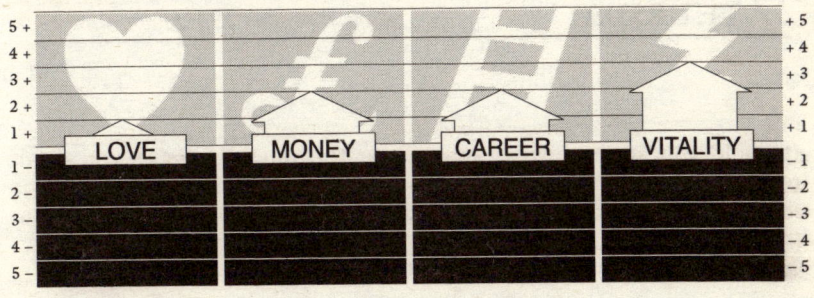

24 MONDAY

Moon Age Day 12   Moon Sign Aquarius

am . . . .

pm . . . .

This ought to be a very positive and dynamic start to the working week for most Aquarians. Not only do you have the ability to get things done yourself, you can also be very inspiring to have around. This should assist you to keep your popularity high and take centre stage in almost all situations.

25 TUESDAY

Moon Age Day 13   Moon Sign Pisces

am . . . .

pm . . . .

Much of the fulfilment you can achieve today lies in private and domestic matters. It probably won't be possible for you to remove yourself from the real world altogether, even if that is what you feel like doing at times. This could be a response to the very active and even breakneck period you have experienced since Saturday.

26 WEDNESDAY

Moon Age Day 14   Moon Sign Pisces

am . . . .

pm . . . .

There are major life decisions to be made and you are in the best possible position to deal with them at this time. You can afford to show a generally happy face to the world and can make light of minor worries, both for yourself and on behalf of others. A day to keep well in touch with relatives who are away from home at present.

27 THURSDAY

Moon Age Day 15   Moon Sign Aries

am . . . .

pm . . . .

It could appear that others are making too much of issues you don't really think are important. Why not stretch your imagination and see things from their point of view? Socially speaking you should keep life as simple as you can, associating freely with just about anyone who comes along and chatting at every opportunity.

28 FRIDAY
Moon Age Day 16   Moon Sign Aries

am . . . .

pm . . . .
Your powers of attraction should be very noticeable today. Getting along with others could prove to be easier than ever, and this relates especially to superiors or those who have influence. Once the concerns of the working day are over you have a chance to commit yourself more to your partner and to family matters.

29 SATURDAY
Moon Age Day 17   Moon Sign Taurus

am . . . .

pm . . . .
Trends now offer a period of escapism. This isn't too unusual for Aquarius, but you need to be careful that you are not neglecting important jobs you have already started. All the same there is nothing wrong with being a dreamer now and again. You might even arrive at some significant realisations.

30 SUNDAY
Moon Age Day 18   Moon Sign Taurus

am . . . .

pm . . . .
There are great opportunities around now for broadening your horizons in a general sense. Whether or not you choose to actually do anything specific today remains to be seen. Don't be afraid to grab with both hands any chance to do something different and to show a positive response to suggestions friends are making.

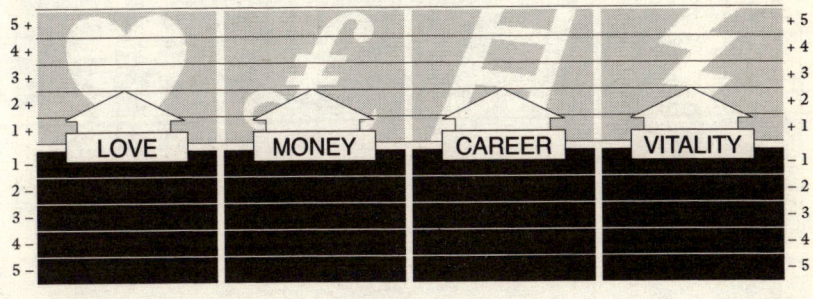

October 2007

YOUR MONTH AT A GLANCE

⊕ = Opportunities are around   ⊖ = Be on the defensive   ⬤ = Life is pretty ordinary

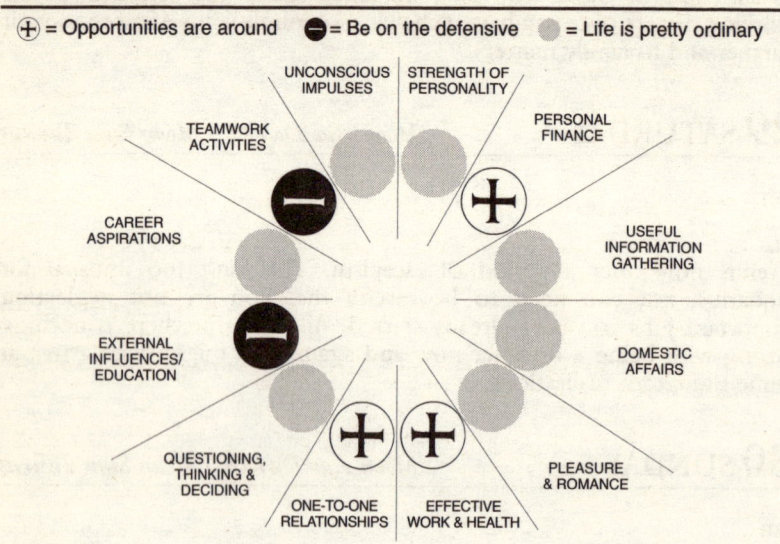

UNCONSCIOUS IMPULSES

STRENGTH OF PERSONALITY

TEAMWORK ACTIVITIES

PERSONAL FINANCE

CAREER ASPIRATIONS

USEFUL INFORMATION GATHERING

EXTERNAL INFLUENCES/ EDUCATION

DOMESTIC AFFAIRS

QUESTIONING, THINKING & DECIDING

ONE-TO-ONE RELATIONSHIPS

EFFECTIVE WORK & HEALTH

PLEASURE & ROMANCE

OCTOBER HIGHS AND LOWS

Here I show you how the rhythms of the Moon will affect you this month. Like the tide, your energies and abilities will rise and fall with its pattern. When it is above the centre line, go for it, when it is below, you should be resting.

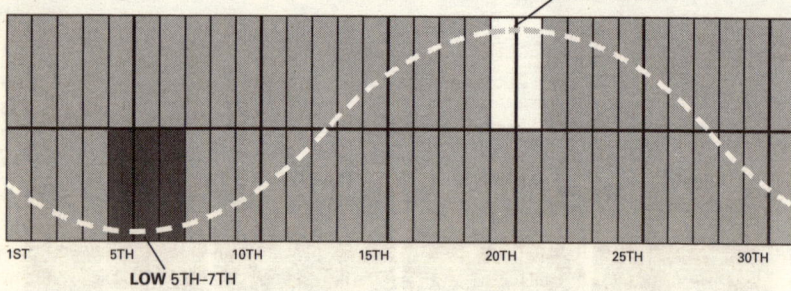

HIGH 20TH–21ST

1ST   5TH   10TH   15TH   20TH   25TH   30TH

LOW 5TH–7TH

1 MONDAY   *Moon Age Day 19   Moon Sign Gemini*

am . . . .

pm . . . .
New information can help you to be fully in the picture today and allows
you to make progress in many different areas of your life. However, much
of what stands around you is only potential, and much depends on your
own efforts. Fortunately there are some very supportive planetary
influences around this week.

2 TUESDAY   *Moon Age Day 20   Moon Sign Gemini*

am . . . .

pm . . . .
It would be good to spread your influence socially and there is certainly
no need to fall out with anyone, even though you might be quite touchy
on occasions. Social trends remain generally positive, though you may
decide to turn more and more to family members in order to fill your
quiet hours at present.

3 WEDNESDAY   *Moon Age Day 21   Moon Sign Cancer*

am . . . .

pm . . . .
Work and career issues have potential to keep you on the go now, in fact
there may not be enough time to do everything that you would wish.
Today responds best if you keep an open mind when it comes to changes
that are now on the cards and don't spend too much time worrying
about what might happen. Most decisions will be yours to make.

4 THURSDAY   *Moon Age Day 22   Moon Sign Cancer*

am . . . .

pm . . . .
A day to keep your mind sharp and to make sure you know what you
want at the moment. You can afford to speak your mind and leave few
people in any doubt about your intentions. As the day grows older you
may notice that you are growing quieter and more in need of moments
for reflection.

5 FRIDAY

Moon Age Day 23   Moon Sign Leo

am . . . .

pm . . . .
Only moderate advancement is indicated today. With the Moon in your solar sixth house the lunar low has arrived. Allow yourself moments of reflection and spend time with loved ones, particularly those who have a need of you at present. This might be a fairly quiet sort of Friday by your usual standards.

6 SATURDAY

Moon Age Day 24   Moon Sign Leo

am . . . .

pm . . . .
You can expect a mixed bag this weekend. Although the lunar low might seem to be putting pressure on you in one way or another, there are sufficient positive aspects around today to help you to overcome its worst influences. In particular you have scope to revel in the company of people you find to be intelligent and stimulating.

7 SUNDAY

Moon Age Day 25   Moon Sign Leo

am . . . .

pm . . . .
The Moon is still in Leo, though its influence there is waning significantly, and if there are any problems around today you can deal with them quickly and efficiently. Romance is an important factor in the lives of many Aquarians at the moment, with the position of the planet Venus offering a real boost to affairs of the heart.

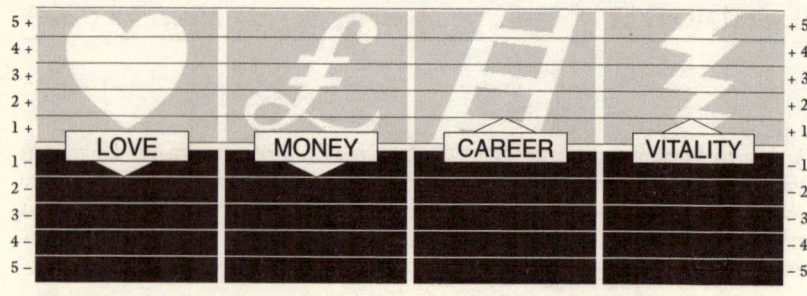

8 MONDAY
Moon Age Day 26   Moon Sign Virgo

am . . . .

pm . . . .
There may be some important things to do today, though they might not turn out to be quite as simple as you might wish. Still, it is possible to apply a little concentration, just as long as you don't try to tackle too many tasks at the same time. Communication counts for a great deal later in the day.

9 TUESDAY
Moon Age Day 27   Moon Sign Virgo

am . . . .

pm . . . .
Restlessness is possible today, but if you are wise you can turn it to your advantage. When it comes to discussions or arguments you might decide to back down, either because you recognise it is not in your best interests to question someone or simply because you want a simple life.

10 WEDNESDAY
Moon Age Day 28   Moon Sign Libra

am . . . .

pm . . . .
Today marks a potentially busy time when you can still find moments for contemplation and for getting your head round problems that might have been with you for a while. Even casual conversations can offer significant clues as to your way forward in a practical sense, and meanwhile you could find love to be inviting.

11 THURSDAY
Moon Age Day 0   Moon Sign Libra

am . . . .

pm . . . .
It would be better by far today to do what you have to do in your own way. Inventing new ways of going about tasks you already understand could well lead to problems further down the line. Your communication skills are certainly not in doubt and your intuition works to your advantage if you listen to it.

12 FRIDAY   ☿   *Moon Age Day 1   Moon Sign Libra*

am . . . .

pm . . . .
Along comes an influx of social invitations and some of these could
detract from your ability to concentrate on strictly practical matters when
they matter the most. Never mind, you can make this an interesting
period all the same, and being an Aquarian you can make the most of the
stimulus that comes from interacting with others.

13 SATURDAY   ☿   *Moon Age Day 2   Moon Sign Scorpio*

am . . . .

pm . . . .
Saturday offers you scope to make contact with types who can be of
specific use to you practically, though by later in the day you may well be
opting for fun. You won't be able to take anyone quite as seriously as
would sometimes be the case and this even includes yourself.

14 SUNDAY   ☿   *Moon Age Day 3   Moon Sign Scorpio*

am . . . .

pm . . . .
Trends encourage you to get more involved in domestic matters than has
been possible for a week or so. You can turn your mind towards the needs
that loved ones have of you and use much of your spare time to make
others feel more secure. Don't be afraid to leave a few moments just for
yourself and take some time out to meditate.

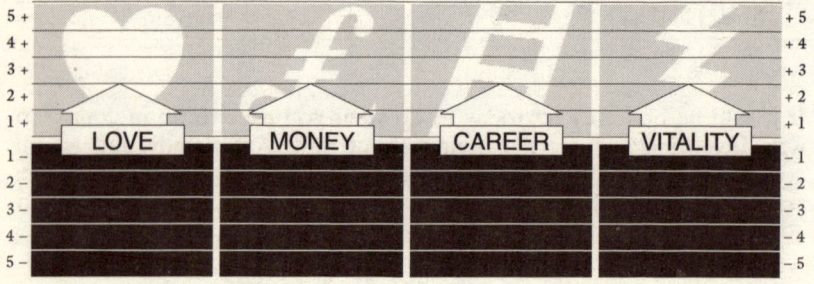

15 MONDAY   ☿   *Moon Age Day 4   Moon Sign Sagittarius*

am . . . .

pm . . . .
Finding the best qualities in others is quite natural to you, though it is a quality that is much enhanced right now. You have what it takes to turn heads and should also notice how much influence you have on those who are in positions of authority. You get your own way best now by using persuasion and not by arguing.

16 TUESDAY   ☿   *Moon Age Day 5   Moon Sign Sagittarius*

am . . . .

pm . . . .
In terms of money you can take advantage of a fairly stable period and one that will allow you to deal with financial matters in a positive way. The real prospects for gain seem to be at work, and you have all it takes to make a good impression. You needn't let any limitations be placed upon you at the moment.

17 WEDNESDAY   ☿   *Moon Age Day 6   Moon Sign Sagittarius*

am . . . .

pm . . . .
Even if there is plenty in the practical world to demand your attention, you could also be quite restless and anxious to ring the changes whenever you can. Friendship proves important at this stage and you have scope to turn to your best pals in order to get information that will help you to move forward.

18 THURSDAY   ☿   *Moon Age Day 7   Moon Sign Capricorn*

am . . . .

pm . . . .
You can be extremely persuasive under present planetary trends and should have very little difficulty persuading others to follow your lead. This can be especially useful at work, where you can use it to put yourself in the running for advancement of some sort. The world tends to be the way you make it right now, so think big!

19 FRIDAY
☿   *Moon Age Day 8*   *Moon Sign Capricorn*

am . . . .

pm . . . .
Things will probably slow just a little as the Moon finishes its pass through your solar twelfth house. This is invariably a time during which you can withdraw somewhat, though you may not be quiet as the day advances and the Moon moves closer to your own zodiac sign of Aquarius.

20 SATURDAY
☿   *Moon Age Day 9*   *Moon Sign Aquarius*

am . . . .

pm . . . .
New starts are there for the taking as the Moon races back into your own zodiac sign, from where it offers better luck, a very positive attitude and much assistance from others. Gains are possible financially and personally, even if you have to look around carefully in order to recognise one or two of them.

21 SUNDAY
☿   *Moon Age Day 10*   *Moon Sign Aquarius*

am . . . .

pm . . . .
You have what it takes to remain ahead of the game most of the time and shouldn't have any real difficulty getting others to do what you think is best. With silver-tongued eloquence you prove just how wonderful the average Aquarian can be at getting his or her own way, and can also capitalise on some particularly good news.

	LOVE	MONEY	CAREER	VITALITY	
5 +					+ 5
4 +					+ 4
3 +					+ 3
2 +					+ 2
1 +					+ 1
1 –					– 1
2 –					– 2
3 –					– 3
4 –					– 4
5 –					– 5

22 MONDAY ☿ *Moon Age Day 11   Moon Sign Pisces*

am . . . .

pm . . . .
Trends remain positive for you in a social sense now, and getting on with people who were difficult a few days ago should be quite easy. If routines are tiresome, your best approach is to ignore them if you can. Artistically you should be on top form and may decide this is a good time for planning changes at home.

23 TUESDAY ☿ *Moon Age Day 12   Moon Sign Pisces*

am . . . .

pm . . . .
Perhaps you should not expect everything in life to suit you today, though the majority of situations should work out fine. Routines might be somewhat hard to establish and as is so often the case for you, there is a great temptation to throw the instruction book out of the window and to 'wing it'.

24 WEDNESDAY ☿ *Moon Age Day 13   Moon Sign Pisces*

am . . . .

pm . . . .
There is one specific piece of advice that really matters today: get organised! You really do need to be on the ball and to prove to everyone around you that you know what you are doing and that you have a plan. Once people see that you are not simply bluffing your way through situations, co-operation should be assured.

25 THURSDAY ☿ *Moon Age Day 14   Moon Sign Aries*

am . . . .

pm . . . .
As is so often the case for Aquarius it is very important to keep your eyes open and to make the most of information that comes your way. Getting an early start would help a great deal, particularly if there is a lot to get done. Tackling half a dozen jobs at the same time is no real drawback as far as you are concerned.

26 FRIDAY ☿ *Moon Age Day 15 Moon Sign Aries*

am . . . .

pm . . . .
Intimate relationships offer promising moments and should help you to
end the working week in a very favourable way. You have what it takes to
win hearts and so if there is someone around you have been wishing to
sweep off their feet, it seems as though this would be the best time of all
to give it a go.

27 SATURDAY ☿ *Moon Age Day 16 Moon Sign Taurus*

am . . . .

pm . . . .
This is a time to show your ingenious nature working at its best. Socially
speaking you can enjoy a fairly easy-going sort of weekend and may not
wish to be involved in lengthy or deep conversations of any sort. Proving
what a party animal you are shouldn't be difficult, because you can
enliven any event.

28 SUNDAY ☿ *Moon Age Day 17 Moon Sign Taurus*

am . . . .

pm . . . .
You need to keep things varied today. The more change and diversity you
get into your life, the better you are likely to enjoy what this Sunday has
to offer. Why not leave all serious issues until another day and show how
spontaneous you can be? You can also gain by simply being in the right
place at the best time.

	LOVE	MONEY	CAREER	VITALITY

29 MONDAY ☿ *Moon Age Day 18 Moon Sign Gemini*

am . . . .

pm . . . .
You would be wise to keep emotional issues at arm's length for the moment and avoid getting bogged down with serious discussions. You have scope to keep life light and airy and that is certainly the best way forward for you at present. Creative potential is good and so is your ability to find new ways to tackle jobs you have been doing for years.

30 TUESDAY ☿ *Moon Age Day 19 Moon Sign Gemini*

am . . . .

pm . . . .
Even if it isn't always easy today to see a point of view you basically don't understand, it's only a matter of time before explanations are available. It is probable that there are some happenings taking place right now to which you cannot be a party for the moment. Try to curb your natural curiosity a little.

31 WEDNESDAY ☿ *Moon Age Day 20 Moon Sign Cancer*

am . . . .

pm . . . .
You may find yourself having to be content with only moderate success in a practical or work sense, but once the responsibility is out of the way you should discover a day that is potentially rewarding. Romance is beginning to show more clearly in the Aquarian life and there are also rewards available as a result of past efforts.

1 THURSDAY ☿ *Moon Age Day 21 Moon Sign Cancer*

am . . . .

pm . . . .
There are signs that the first day of November could find you somewhat grumpy. The fact that the year is advancing so fast and in fact has nearly reached its end is hardly likely to inspire you. This is probably because you expect so much of yourself that it would be almost impossible to have everything you would wish.

2 FRIDAY ☿ *Moon Age Day 22   Moon Sign Leo*

am . . . .

pm . . . .
With the lunar low present this would hardly be the best time for taking any sort of risk. In the main your best approach is to keep a generally low profile and to be content with your own company for at least part of the time. All Aquarians can use today as a significantly quieter interlude than would normally be the case.

3 SATURDAY *Moon Age Day 23   Moon Sign Leo*

am . . . .

pm . . . .
Getting what you want most is possible today, though you would have to work so hard to achieve your objectives that you would exhaust yourself. On the other hand, you do have what it takes to get others to do things on your behalf. They think they are working towards their own objectives – but you, of course, know different!

4 SUNDAY *Moon Age Day 24   Moon Sign Virgo*

am . . . .

pm . . . .
Look out for new friendships on the horizon, a fact that may well please you at a time when present attachments might be in doubt. Don't be too worried if you can't get family members to follow your instructions today. It's worth leaving them to their own devices and getting on with what is important to you, now the lunar low is out of the way.

5 +			+ 5
4 +			+ 4
3 +			+ 3
2 +			+ 2
1 +			+ 1
LOVE	MONEY	CAREER	VITALITY
1 −			− 1
2 −			− 2
3 −			− 3
4 −			− 4
5 −			− 5

November
2007

YOUR MONTH AT A GLANCE

⊕ = Opportunities are around   ⊖ = Be on the defensive   ⬤ = Life is pretty ordinary

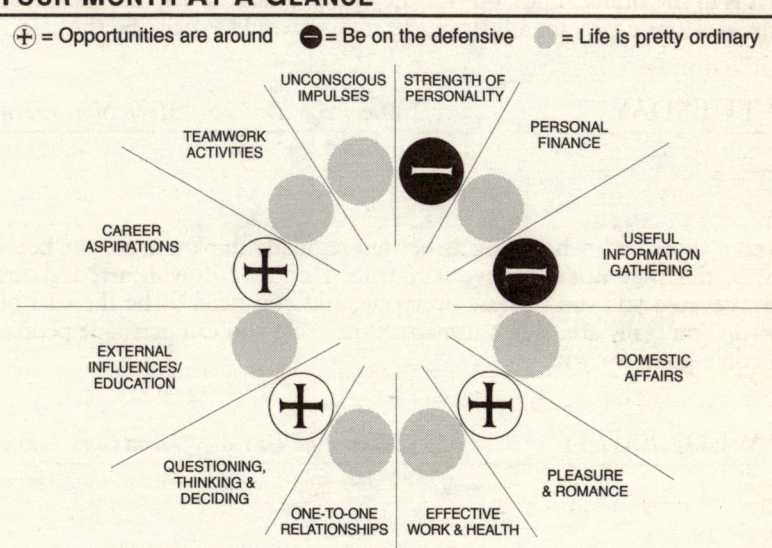

- UNCONSCIOUS IMPULSES
- STRENGTH OF PERSONALITY ⊖
- PERSONAL FINANCE
- TEAMWORK ACTIVITIES
- CAREER ASPIRATIONS ⊕
- USEFUL INFORMATION GATHERING ⊖
- EXTERNAL INFLUENCES/ EDUCATION
- DOMESTIC AFFAIRS
- QUESTIONING, THINKING & DECIDING ⊕
- PLEASURE & ROMANCE ⊕
- ONE-TO-ONE RELATIONSHIPS
- EFFECTIVE WORK & HEALTH

NOVEMBER HIGHS AND LOWS

Here I show you how the rhythms of the Moon will affect you this month. Like the tide, your energies and abilities will rise and fall with its pattern. When it is above the centre line, go for it, when it is below, you should be resting.

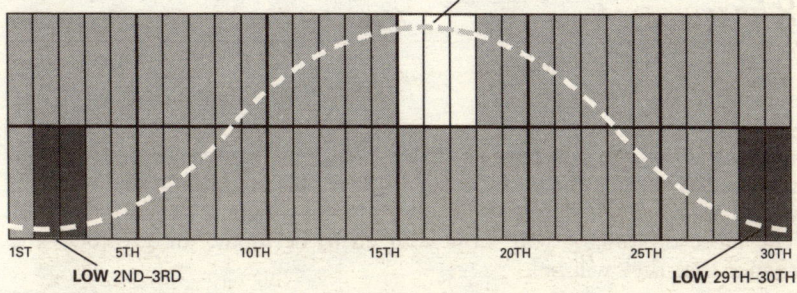

HIGH 16TH–18TH

1ST   5TH   10TH   15TH   20TH   25TH   30TH

LOW 2ND–3RD   **LOW** 29TH–30TH

5 MONDAY
Moon Age Day 25   Moon Sign Virgo

am ....

pm ....
You can make the most of a little luck in the financial sphere around this time, and you need to be on the ball when it comes to any sort of deal that is in the offing. Look out for the odd practical mishap that is maybe caused because you are a little clumsier than would usually be the case.

6 TUESDAY
Moon Age Day 26   Moon Sign Libra

am ....

pm ....
Even if those with whom you associated regularly think you are the bee's knees, this may not be universally true. Don't be downhearted about this, because you can't please everyone, and you need to be the sort of person you really are. When it matters the most you can persuade people to come good for you.

7 WEDNESDAY
Moon Age Day 27   Moon Sign Libra

am ....

pm ....
A day to take a little trip if possible and to make some changes to the routines of your life. It would be all too easy to become bored with things at the moment, and in order to avoid this happening you may have to put in a little extra effort. Consideration for family members counts for a great deal now.

8 THURSDAY
Moon Age Day 28   Moon Sign Libra

am ....

pm ....
It looks as though you have some big ideas now, and you need to do all you can to exploit them. In order to have things running the way you would really wish it might be necessary to get others to do your bidding. The more diplomatic you show yourself to be today, the greater is the chance that they will help.

9 FRIDAY
Moon Age Day 0   Moon Sign Scorpio

am . . . .

pm . . . .
This has potential to be a very split sort of day. Mercury encourages your communicative side, but other planetary influences show that there is also a quieter aspect to your nature. One area of life that should be looking fairly good is romance – so much so that a new attachment is a possibility for some Aquarians.

10 SATURDAY
Moon Age Day 1   Moon Sign Scorpio

am . . . .

pm . . . .
You have scope to get out and about more than ever today and the weekend offers much to those Aquarians who are genuinely willing to put themselves out. There isn't any use in waiting around for anyone else to make the arrangements, and although you will have to work hard to get others involved, the effort should be more than worthwhile.

11 SUNDAY
Moon Age Day 2   Moon Sign Sagittarius

am . . . .

pm . . . .
This would be a very favourable time for all matters to do with holiday arrangements or even for planning a business trip of some sort. There is a degree of restlessness about you at this time and you need to bring some change into your life if you are not to end up feeling rather bored.

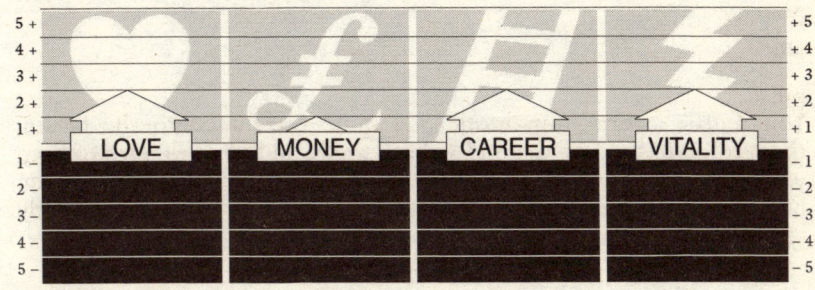

12 MONDAY
Moon Age Day 3   Moon Sign Sagittarius

am . . . .

pm . . . .
Communication with others can be enlivening and even exciting at the start of this new working week. You tend to be acting on impulse for much of the time, but this is so much a part of your basic nature that it isn't any sort of problem. Be prepared to listen to the ideas of a colleague because they could suit you too.

13 TUESDAY
Moon Age Day 4   Moon Sign Sagittarius

am . . . .

pm . . . .
Today responds best if you take every possible opportunity to get away from the ordinary in life. Winter is here and things can start to look very grey and uninspiring unless you put in that extra bit of effort yourself. Aquarius has the power to lift its own spirits and those of everyone with whom it comes into contact.

14 WEDNESDAY
Moon Age Day 5   Moon Sign Capricorn

am . . . .

pm . . . .
Today can be favourable for career progress, but now that the Moon has entered your solar twelfth house you can also afford to take some time for necessary reflection. In a day or two things could get busy so you may as well take a short break from self-imposed pressure whilst you can.

15 THURSDAY
Moon Age Day 6   Moon Sign Capricorn

am . . . .

pm . . . .
You remain basically optimistic and quite committed to the future, though there could be the odd setback today, and you will need to keep your wits about you if you if you don't want to start again at the beginning with some specific projects. It may be best to settle for a fairly steady day, but that might be too much to expect.

16 FRIDAY — *Moon Age Day 7   Moon Sign Aquarius*

am . . . .

pm . . . .
Just as you were starting to flag a little, along comes the lunar high. There is tremendous incentive to get on with new ideas and schemes and to push forward progressively in most spheres of your life. What you definitely do have right now is popularity, and you could hardly fail to realise the fact.

17 SATURDAY — *Moon Age Day 8   Moon Sign Aquarius*

am . . . .

pm . . . .
You can make this a really good weekend, and with the lunar high pushing from behind you have everything you need to move forward at a significant pace, no matter what you decide to do. Excitement is like food and drink to you at the moment and you need to find something to do that gives you a definite thrill.

18 SUNDAY — *Moon Age Day 9   Moon Sign Aquarius*

am . . . .

pm . . . .
Keep up the pressure to have a good time and to take others along with you. Your company is inspiring and you can make sure you are the star of the show. There may be one or two people who don't think you are quite so wonderful, but that is part of the price paid by all Air-sign individuals such as you.

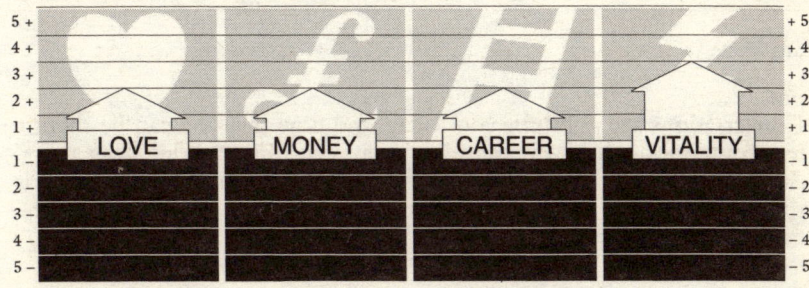

19 MONDAY　　　*Moon Age Day 10　　Moon Sign Pisces*

am . . . .

pm . . . .
Learning new things can be a great deal of fun this week and you can afford to launch yourself into projects with a great deal of enthusiasm. If certain people prove to be difficult, you will have to show great diplomacy if you are to avoid getting into some sort of disagreement or even a downright row.

20 TUESDAY　　　*Moon Age Day 11　　Moon Sign Pisces*

am . . . .

pm . . . .
Don't hesitate today. Things work best for you when you are willing to recognise a challenge and to face up to it immediately. There are definite gains to be made and some of these may be of a financial nature. Routines are out at the moment, partly because you won't have time for them.

21 WEDNESDAY　　　*Moon Age Day 12　　Moon Sign Aries*

am . . . .

pm . . . .
It is possible that you will be somewhat argumentative today, and you need to curb this tendency if you want to avoid falling out with someone who is in a position to do you a great deal of good. Count to ten before you react, and even when you are faced with people you see as being deliberately stupid you need to keep your cool.

22 THURSDAY　　　*Moon Age Day 13　　Moon Sign Aries*

am . . . .

pm . . . .
Conversations are good for you today, and now that you can be slightly less contentious than you were yesterday you can get a lot from them. Aquarius tends to act on impulse for much of the time and it looks as though today will be no exception. Why not save some time in the evening to please your partner?

144

23 FRIDAY
Moon Age Day 14   Moon Sign Taurus

am . . . .

pm . . . .
This should prove to be one of the better days of the month during
which to enjoy friendship and the simple things of life. If you feel a bit
lacking in lustre all you probably need is a temporary change of scene.
When a particular task gets boring or frustrating, don't be afraid to put
it aside for a while.

24 SATURDAY
Moon Age Day 15   Moon Sign Taurus

am . . . .

pm . . . .
Aquarians who work at the weekend should find today to be very useful,
but even if your time is your own you shouldn't have any trouble filling
it. Now is the time to get in step with friends and do something quite out
of the ordinary if you can. Your worst enemy at the moment is boredom,
and you need to be inventive to avoid it.

25 SUNDAY
Moon Age Day 16   Moon Sign Gemini

am . . . .

pm . . . .
Family and domestic situations are highlighted today. It's worth getting
together with your loved ones and making some plans for the future. It
is possible that one of your chief concerns will be Christmas, which is
only a month away. When it comes to domestic chores, do your best to
be inventive and to change the order in which you do things.

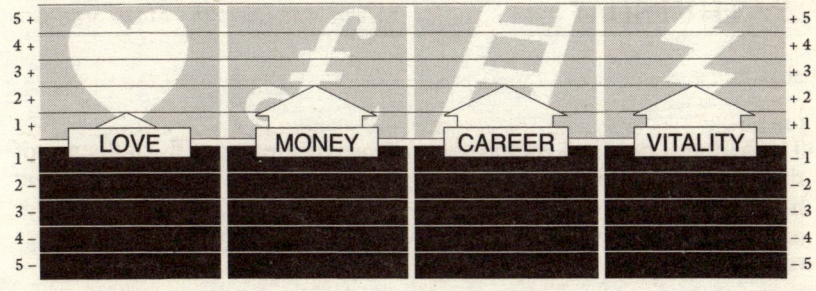

26 MONDAY   *Moon Age Day 17   Moon Sign Gemini*

am . . . .

pm . . . .
You can now change the way you communicate with others. It may be
that you are being much more selective in the people you approach, and
you might also be happy to leave alone those who regularly cause
problems for you. Aquarius could be just a little more selfish than usual
right now.

27 TUESDAY   *Moon Age Day 18   Moon Sign Cancer*

am . . . .

pm . . . .
Trends offer you a relaxing and interesting sort of day but also a time
during which you can think deeply about an issue that has been on your
mind for some time. If you remain relaxed you can now deal with
situations better and can find answers that have eluded you for a few
weeks or even months.

28 WEDNESDAY   *Moon Age Day 19   Moon Sign Cancer*

am . . . .

pm . . . .
Whenever it proves to be possible you need to widen your horizons.
Don't just look at the possible, but seek to stretch yourself whenever you
can. The tendency to feel bored by life is still hovering around and you
need to do everything you can to counteract this trend. Seeking out
interesting people and new situations can work wonders.

29 THURSDAY   *Moon Age Day 20   Moon Sign Leo*

am . . . .

pm . . . .
The Moon is now in Leo and that means you are under the influence of
the lunar low. With some strong supporting planetary influences you may
hardly notice the less positive aspects of this time, though a quieter
interlude is possible, offering you a chance to spend more hours on your
own than would usually be the case.

30 FRIDAY
Moon Age Day 21   Moon Sign Leo

am . . . .

pm . . . .
Even if you decide to slow down the current pace of events, that doesn't mean you have to stop altogether. What is really necessary is more concentration on specific matters, whilst you leave others to sort out routine jobs. Support from family members can prove to be especially useful around this time.

1 SATURDAY
Moon Age Day 22   Moon Sign Virgo

am . . . .

pm . . . .
The start of December brings situations that could take you by surprise. Most of these are likely to be positive in nature and offer you an opportunity to reap the benefits of efforts you have put in previously. You have what it takes to put the warmest and most endearing qualities of your nature on display this weekend.

2 SUNDAY
Moon Age Day 23   Moon Sign Virgo

am . . . .

pm . . . .
Whilst you are definitely on the move again you would be wise to exercise just a little care today. There are new people to meet and exciting situations to address. The only slight fly in the ointment is the way you approach both people and events. Avoid coming on too strong and be as 'cool' as you can.

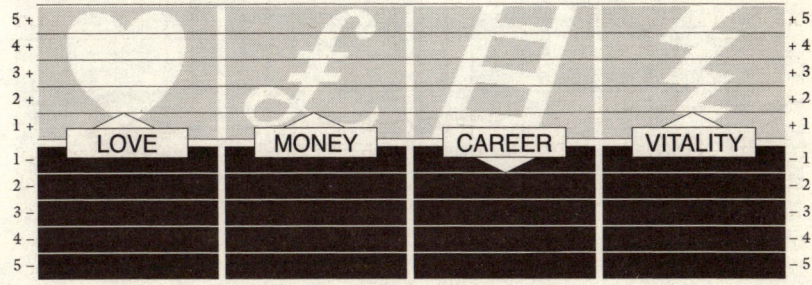

December
2007

YOUR MONTH AT A GLANCE

⊕ = Opportunities are around   ⊖ = Be on the defensive   ⬤ = Life is pretty ordinary

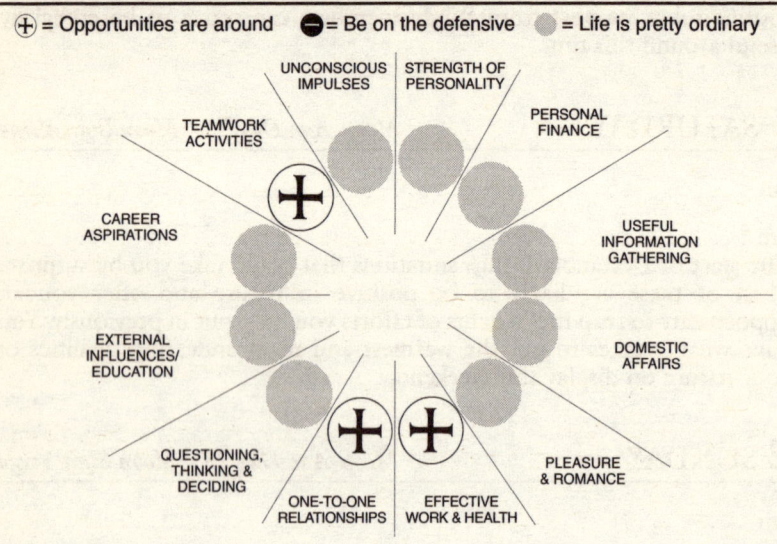

- UNCONSCIOUS IMPULSES
- STRENGTH OF PERSONALITY
- TEAMWORK ACTIVITIES
- PERSONAL FINANCE
- CAREER ASPIRATIONS
- USEFUL INFORMATION GATHERING
- EXTERNAL INFLUENCES/ EDUCATION
- DOMESTIC AFFAIRS
- QUESTIONING, THINKING & DECIDING
- ONE-TO-ONE RELATIONSHIPS
- EFFECTIVE WORK & HEALTH
- PLEASURE & ROMANCE

DECEMBER HIGHS AND LOWS

Here I show you how the rhythms of the Moon will affect you this month. Like the tide, your energies and abilities will rise and fall with its pattern. When it is above the centre line, go for it, when it is below, you should be resting.

HIGH 14TH–15TH

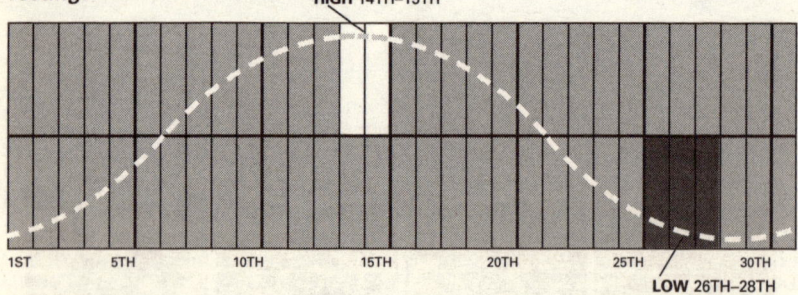

1ST   5TH   10TH   15TH   20TH   25TH   30TH

LOW 26TH–28TH

3 MONDAY
Moon Age Day 24   Moon Sign Virgo

am . . . .

pm . . . .
Even if personal relationships are rather downbeat at present, you need to take your joys where you can find them. Today that means friendship and the support that particular individuals are offering. In a practical sense it would be best not to take anything for granted, especially at work.

4 TUESDAY
Moon Age Day 25   Moon Sign Libra

am . . . .

pm . . . .
Rather than rushing ahead like some people today, being careful is what counts for you. Whilst others have to repeat procedures time and again, you can get them right first time round. Focusing on the small details right now should give you what you need to get in front of the pack.

5 WEDNESDAY
Moon Age Day 26   Moon Sign Libra

am . . . .

pm . . . .
Wednesday should offer a period of swifter progress. If you put on a spurt you can steal a march on someone who has been beating you to the punch, though without upsetting them too much. What matters at present is convincing yourself that you are as capable as you believe yourself to be when you are at your most confident.

6 THURSDAY
Moon Age Day 27   Moon Sign Scorpio

am . . . .

pm . . . .
Be prepared to seek out the company of interesting and witty people right now and to get ahead in ways you haven't been expecting. For all this you can thank a host of small planetary influences, which when working together should help you to focus on an exciting and uncluttered horizon.

7 FRIDAY

Moon Age Day 28   Moon Sign Scorpio

am . . . .

pm . . . .
There are signs that a person higher up the career ladder than you are can steer you in the right direction, if you are only willing to listen to what they say. Reliance on friends can be stronger now and new friendships could be formed around this period. At least part of your mind may now be focused on the Christmas period.

8 SATURDAY

Moon Age Day 29   Moon Sign Scorpio

am . . . .

pm . . . .
The more you put yourself about at the moment, the greater should be your sense of achievement. Although you might not be able to take the starring role in everything, you are unlikely to be moved too much by this fact. By the evening you can afford to have your sights set on interesting social possibilities.

9 SUNDAY

Moon Age Day 0   Moon Sign Sagittarius

am . . . .

pm . . . .
Even if you are in the mood for Christmas shopping today, you would be wise to avoid making spur of the moment purchases and instead, save your money for another day. Why not ask friends for help and advice? Make certain you listen carefully to what they are saying.

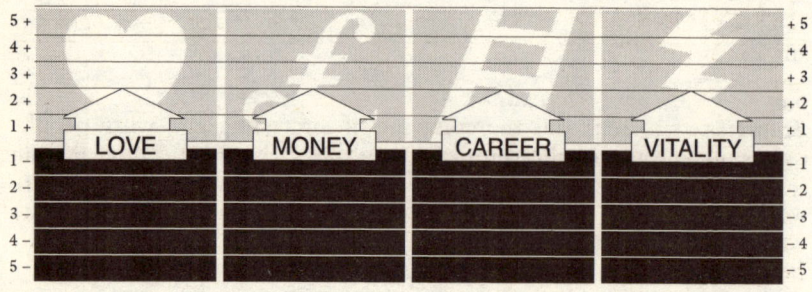

10 MONDAY
Moon Age Day 1   Moon Sign Sagittarius

am . . . .

pm . . . .
Rather than being too tied down with the realities of work today, you have scope to have fun, and can find people who are willing to help you do so. Stay away from negative people, or the sort of individuals who are backbiting and cruel. The closer you are to the people you are dealing with personally, the better you should feel.

11 TUESDAY
Moon Age Day 2   Moon Sign Capricorn

am . . . .

pm . . . .
Taking care of minor details will probably occupy some of your time today, but you should have a broader and more expansive interest in life too. This shows itself in a number of different ways, but as the day wears on you could notice that you are slightly quieter than has been the case for quite a few days.

12 WEDNESDAY
Moon Age Day 3   Moon Sign Capricorn

am . . . .

pm . . . .
A day to take some time out to think things through. If you keep your mind uncluttered with details, you should be able to see clearly through to the heart of most situations. It's worth reassuring those with whom you live that you have been thinking about the festive season and that many of the necessary details are sorted.

13 THURSDAY
Moon Age Day 4   Moon Sign Capricorn

am . . . .

pm . . . .
Personalities tend to enter your life at the moment, or at least that is how it seems. The truth of the matter may be that you are not shining quite so brightly yourself at present and so tend to notice the positive points of others more. The Moon in your solar twelfth house encourages you to be quite contemplative.

14 FRIDAY

Moon Age Day 5   Moon Sign Aquarius

am . . . .

pm . . . .

The most important physical peak of the month comes along now, thanks to the lunar high. For a couple of days you should be feeling extremely fit and willing to take on just about any task that comes your way. Keep as distant as you can from tedious jobs at the moment, sticking instead to what gives you pleasure.

15 SATURDAY

Moon Age Day 6   Moon Sign Aquarius

am . . . .

pm . . . .

The lunar high is still around and there are gains to be made, even in unexpected directions. Money matters ought to be easier and you can make the most of extra energy. Now you really can chance your arm, which is pretty much in line with the Aquarian nature when working at its best.

16 SUNDAY

Moon Age Day 7   Moon Sign Pisces

am . . . .

pm . . . .

Your strength lies in keeping life light and bright and not taking yourself or anyone else more seriously than you have to. The sort of people with whom you choose to mix today need to be individuals who have a good sense of humour and who are willing to make some of the running. You can take delight in interesting conversations.

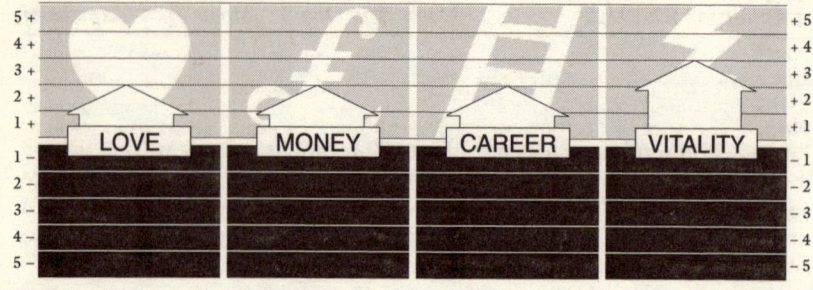

17 MONDAY   *Moon Age Day 8   Moon Sign Pisces*

am . . . .

pm . . . .
Some fairly interesting news may be available now, and this allows you to address your own needs and wishes. Getting on with the task in hand is paramount, but is occasionally difficult with so many distractions coming in from all quarters. You already have one eye on the needs of Christmas.

18 TUESDAY   *Moon Age Day 9   Moon Sign Aries*

am . . . .

pm . . . .
Don't be afraid to take on novel interests at this time and be willing to look at new ways of doing things. There is some good advice around at present, as long as you are willing to look at it with an open mind. Creative potential remains essentially good, so now might be a good time to put up the tree and the decorations.

19 WEDNESDAY   *Moon Age Day 10   Moon Sign Aries*

am . . . .

pm . . . .
Stronger than normal ego tendencies are possible under present trends. You might be taking on rather too much just now and a little fresh air would do you good. You need some space to think things through and to put the brakes on your present tendency to lord it slightly over others. This isn't usual for Aquarius.

20 THURSDAY   *Moon Age Day 11   Moon Sign Taurus*

am . . . .

pm . . . .
Even if the sort of excitement you seem to be looking for at the moment is absent, you can make it for yourself if you are willing to put in that extra bit of effort. You can persuade relatives and friends to join in and can dream up some novel ways to entertain both them and yourself.

21 FRIDAY
Moon Age Day 12   Moon Sign Taurus

am . . . .

pm . . . .
Your powers of attraction are strong right now, and that can prove to be very useful. The bearing you have on the thinking processes of those around you may be quite surprising, and could lead you to taking the odd risk when dealing with your partner or sweetheart. In at least one matter you can afford to throw caution to the wind.

22 SATURDAY
Moon Age Day 13   Moon Sign Gemini

am . . . .

pm . . . .
As a direct contrast to yesterday, personal relationships might not appear to be doing you too much in the way of favours today. As a result you may decide to concentrate more on friends than on your partner or family members. A word of caution – with Christmas so close this is no time to be taking on too much in terms of new projects.

23 SUNDAY
Moon Age Day 14   Moon Sign Gemini

am . . . .

pm . . . .
This would be a good day for asking questions and for gathering new information about life and the part you play in it. Be careful with last-minute shopping. It's possible that you could be fooled into thinking that you are getting a bargain, when you know in your heart that you are being conned.

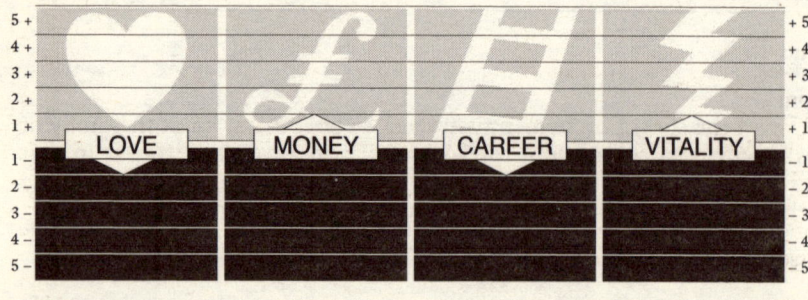

24 MONDAY   *Moon Age Day 15   Moon Sign Cancer*

am . . . .

pm . . . .
There are signs that getting stuck with mundane routines won't appeal
to you very much at all now. On the contrary you are more likely to be
busy in a practical sense and away from home for at least some of the
time. If people are relying heavily on you, the pressure you are under
might begin to show at some stage.

25 TUESDAY   *Moon Age Day 16   Moon Sign Cancer*

am . . . .

pm . . . .
You can make Christmas Day a huge hoot, though you may begin to flag
later in the day. If there is a journey to be made, why not get it out of the
way early and then find time to sit down and put your feet up? What
shows most clearly throughout the whole day is how well your sense of
humour goes down with those around you.

26 WEDNESDAY   *Moon Age Day 17   Moon Sign Leo*

am . . . .

pm . . . .
Boxing Day may well bring a lessening of the amount of energy at your
disposal. This really is the sort of day when you ought to be thinking
about simple pleasures and good company. Being an Aquarian you are
probably on the go for most of the time, so there is nothing wrong at all
with taking a break.

27 THURSDAY   *Moon Age Day 18   Moon Sign Leo*

am . . . .

pm . . . .
The Moon is still in Leo and that means the lunar low can have a bearing
on your attitudes and actions. As New Year approaches you can get
yourself right back on form, but for the moment you can make the most
of this opportunity to watch and wait. Anything with an artistic
association has potential to please you today.

28 FRIDAY
Moon Age Day 19   Moon Sign Leo

am . . . .

pm . . . .
Although you begin today with the Moon in Leo, by the afternoon the planetary situation will have changed markedly. You might begin to wonder why you have been so lethargic and will rapidly make sure you become the life and soul of any party that is in the offing. A day to show real support for any relative or friend who is in need.

29 SATURDAY
Moon Age Day 20   Moon Sign Virgo

am . . . .

pm . . . .
This is a day when you should be prepared to let everyone know exactly who you are. Once you have decided on a particular course of action at present, you can afford to stick with it to the bitter end. New Year resolutions should already be on your mind, and you might even be putting some of them into action early.

30 SUNDAY
Moon Age Day 21   Moon Sign Virgo

am . . . .

pm . . . .
Today is an excellent time for social get-togethers of almost any sort. If you are willing to mix business with pleasure you can help yourself no end and could even end up gaining in ways that are really surprising. Your naturally friendly ways are fully on display and you can use them to get you some special favours.

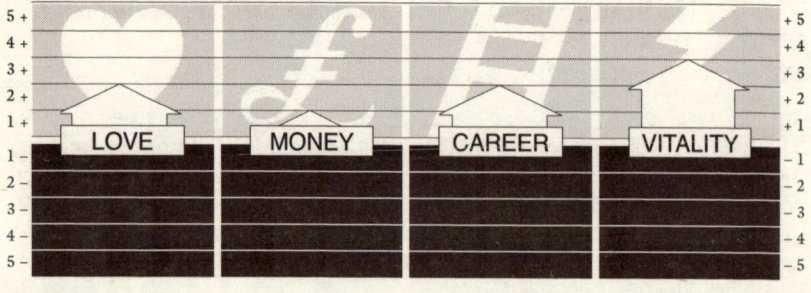

31 MONDAY

Moon Age Day 22   Moon Sign Libra

am . . . .

pm . . . .
There are some great things happening on the social horizon and you ought to be in a good position to gain from them today. Any slight frustration that the holidays are preventing you from getting ahead in more practical ways should soon be forgotten once you decide to immerse yourself in the New Year celebrations.

RISING SIGNS FOR AQUARIUS

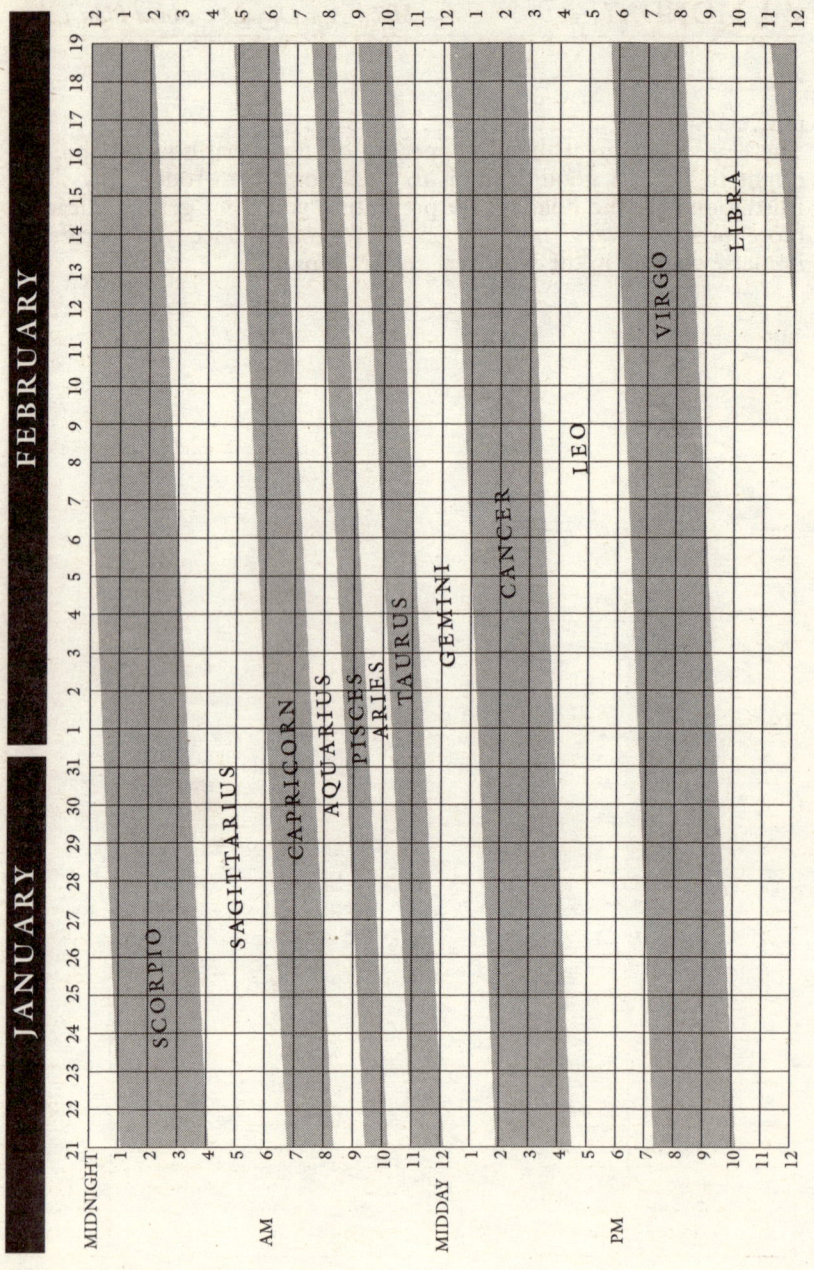

THE ZODIAC, PLANETS AND CORRESPONDENCES

The Earth revolves around the Sun once every calendar year, so when viewed from Earth the Sun appears in a different part of the sky as the year progresses. In astrology, these parts of the sky are divided into the signs of the zodiac and this means that the signs are organised in a circle. The circle begins with Aries and ends with Pisces.

Taking the zodiac sign as a starting point, astrologers then work with all the positions of planets, stars and many other factors to calculate horoscopes and birth charts and tell us what the stars have in store for us.

The table below shows the planets and Elements for each of the signs of the zodiac. Each sign belongs to one of the four Elements: Fire, Air, Earth or Water. Fire signs are creative and enthusiastic; Air signs are mentally active and thoughtful; Earth signs are constructive and practical; Water signs are emotional and have strong feelings.

It also shows the metals and gemstones associated with, or corresponding with, each sign. The correspondence is made when a metal or stone possesses properties that are held in common with a particular sign of the zodiac.

Finally, the table shows the opposite of each star sign – this is the opposite sign in the astrological circle.

Placed	Sign	Symbol	Element	Planet	Metal	Stone	Opposite
1	Aries	Ram	Fire	Mars	Iron	Bloodstone	Libra
2	Taurus	Bull	Earth	Venus	Copper	Sapphire	Scorpio
3	Gemini	Twins	Air	Mercury	Mercury	Tiger's Eye	Sagittarius
4	Cancer	Crab	Water	Moon	Silver	Pearl	Capricorn
5	Leo	Lion	Fire	Sun	Gold	Ruby	Aquarius
6	Virgo	Maiden	Earth	Mercury	Mercury	Sardonyx	Pisces
7	Libra	Scales	Air	Venus	Copper	Sapphire	Aries
8	Scorpio	Scorpion	Water	Pluto	Plutonium	Jasper	Taurus
9	Sagittarius	Archer	Fire	Jupiter	Tin	Topaz	Gemini
10	Capricorn	Goat	Earth	Saturn	Lead	Black Onyx	Cancer
11	Aquarius	Waterbearer	Air	Uranus	Uranium	Amethyst	Leo
12	Pisces	Fishes	Water	Neptune	Tin	Moonstone	Virgo

Foulsham books can be found in all
good bookshops or direct from
www.foulsham.com